Never Throw Stones At Your Mother

Irish Insults and Curses

First published by Appletree Press Ltd,
The Old Potato Station, 14 Howard Street South,
Belfast, BT7 1AP
Tel: +44 (0) 28 90 243074
Fax: +44 (0) 28 90 246756
E-mail: reception@appletree.ie
Web Site: www.irelandseye.com

Never Throw Stones at Your Mother
Irish Insults and Curses

ISBN 0-86281-779-X

A catalogue record for this book is available
from the British Library.

9 8 7 6 5 4 3 2 1

NEVER THROW STONES
AT YOUR MOTHER —

∏ever Throw Stones At Your Mother

Irish Insults and Curses

David Ross

"The everlasting quotation-lover dotes on the husks of learning. He is the infant-reciting bore in second-childishness."

Maria Edgeworth, Thoughts on Bores

"conduct which combines the inaccuracy of the eavesdropper with the method of the blackmailer."

Oscar Wilde, to a collector of anecdotes

Contents

Introduction

The insult in Ireland has a long and lethal history. In the old heroic
Celtic world, the most-feared man was not the champion warrior with his
helmet and spear. Even the most ferocious of fighting men walked warily
when the satirist was in sight. In that society, proud, jealous, brilliantly
articulate, a sharp dismissive phrase from one of the *filidh* could destroy a
hero's reputation and ruin a lifetime's reputation for honest slaughtering
and rapine. From its beginnings in ancient times, this tradition survived
into the historical period. Vivian Mercier, in *The Irish Comic Tradition*
(1962) noted that: "In 1414, as we are informed by the Four Masters,
Niall O'Higgins, a famous poet of Westmeath, composed a satire for Sir
John Higgins, Lord Lieutenant of Ireland, which caused his death."

Irish insults are not to be trifled with, even today. In a country which sets
a high value on the art of conversation, vivid and expressive phrases are
cherished and admired. (Often, too, we might suspect they are rehearsed
in advance – but there is also plenty of high-speed repartee recorded in
this book). The nation of Swift and Wilde, Sheridan and Shaw, has a high
standing in the world league of Insult and Invective. Here as in some
other areas of creative thought, Ireland has always punched far above her
weight. Why should this be so?

The Celtic legacy is undoubtedly important here. Our ancestors knew and
relished the value of words. The culture was public and open: people did
not sit alone to read (most of them could not read) or listen to music.
Stories, songs, history were public events. Praise, blame or shame, everything was shared with the neighbours. This often required some tact and
delicacy on the part of the bard: his audience were a proud and touchy
lot. An aspersion cast on a remote ancestor would be taken as a slur on
his descendants. To balance such carefulness and restraint, the insult
became both natural and necessary. Within the tribal group, the verbal
daggers might be sheathed most of the time; those outside were fair game.
As there were more than a hundred little kingdoms in these days, there
was plenty of opportunity to poke fun at "them". The later history of

Ireland, as she became aware of her large and imperialistic neighbour, offered an even bigger and softer target. As far as the English were concerned, the Irish had plenty to complain about, and they were not reticent. The English, of course, have never been slow to pass comment on their neighbours, and this collection also includes some notable insults to Ireland and the Irish over the centuries.

In more recent times, the Irish art of insult has been turned to all manner of things, as a glance through the 'One-off Judgements' section in this book will show. But no target – not the English, not the Americans – has ever been quite so tempting to the Irish as themselves. Some commentators see in this the evidence that tribalism has not disappeared but simply taken new forms. Others see the whole country as if it were one gigantic village where everyone is looking out at everyone else, busy begrudging and disapproving of them. Whatever the truth of it, it is rich ground for the germination of insult and invective.

Lest there should be any misunderstanding, it must be said emphatically that this collection has not been made to re-open old wounds or cause new offence. There is a vast amount of humour and wit contained in insult and invective, and the best insults live on after the anger has evaporated. The aim here is to entertain, and perhaps occasionally to provoke a little wry reflection. You can learn a lot about a people from their cursings.

Actors and the Theatre

In the eighteenth century, Margaret 'Peg' Woffington, born in Dublin, was a fine actress with a busy social life. When she played Sir Harry Wildair in Farquhar's *The Constant Couple*, she confided to a colleague, James Quin, that half the population really believed she was a man. "Madam," replied Quin, "the other half knows you to be a woman."

The same Quin one day complained of his old age and infirmity, to some friends in Bath.
"What would you give, sir, to be as young as I am?" asked one pert youth.
"Why sir,' said Quin, 'I should almost consent to be as foolish."
(The same anecdote is told about others, including Dr Samuel Johnson)

When the actress Mrs Patrick Campbell was rehearsing his *Pygmalion,* and George Bernard Shaw was taking issue with her rendering of her part, she strode to the front of the stage and said:
"You are a terrible man, Mr Shaw. One day you'll eat a beefsteak and then God help all women."

One longs for the palmy days of . . . the late Lorcan Bourke, who refused to have a chandelier installed in the Olympic Theatre on the grounds that no-one would know how to play it.
Hugh Leonard (1926-), *The Unimportance of Being Irish,* in *Irishmen in a Changing Society* (1988)

Anew MacMaster was a celebrated actor-manager who took classical theatre to all parts of the country in the mid-twentieth century. His appearance and style were flamboyant. Putting his head out of the window one day at a country railway junction, he inquired of the station-master:
"What country, friend, is this?"
The station-master, who knew his Shakespeare, completed the quotation with a heavy emphasis on the last word:
"This is Illyria, lady."

It is greatly to Mrs Patrick Campbell's credit that, bad as the play was, her acting was worse. It was a masterpiece of failure.
George Bernard Shaw (1856-1950)

She'll turn it into "The Second Mrs Conchobar."
John Millington Synge (1871-1909), on Mrs Patrick Campbell as Deirdre in his *Deirdre of the Sorrows*

In the Abbey Theatre, Mrs Patrick Campbell, having thrown a memorable tantrum during a rehearsal of W. B. Yeats's *Deirdre,* in the presence of the writer, made her way to the footlights, and shouted to him:
"I'd give anything to know what you're thinking."
"I'm thinking," replied Yeats, "of the master of an Indian wayside railway station who sent a message to his Company's headquarters saying: 'Tigress on the line: wire instructions'."

On another occasion, Yeats described Mrs Pat Campbell as having "an ego like a raging tooth."

Authors and Their Work

Willie the Spooks
The Gland Old Man
Dublin epithets for W.B. Yeats, taking up his interest in the occult and in
prophylactic treatments.

"Lallah Rookh" –
Is a naughty book
By Tommy Moore,
Who has written four,
Each warmer
Than the former,
So the most recent,
Is the least decent.
Anonymous, on Thomas Moore (1779-1852)

Thomas Moore and some friends were at the Meeting of the Waters,
admiring the scene, when an elderly tramp came into sight. He
approached Moore and asked for alms. Moore paid no attention to him.
The tramp repeated his request, and Moore turned away. Whereupon the
tramp spoke these words,
"If Moore was a man without place of abode,
Without clothes on his back, and him walking the road,
Without bit in his belly or shoes on his feet,
He would not give a damn where the bright waters meet."
"Repeat it," said Moore, and the tramp did so. The poet put his hand in
his pocket and gave the old man half a sovereign.
"I couldn't have done better myself," he said.

. . . the splendidly mad Irishman . . . who wanted to commit suicide, a
fate he nearly imposed on half the faculty of the Ecole by playing the
flute - an instrument of which he was far from being a master - every
night in his room from midnight to dawn.
Richard Aldington, on Samuel Beckett's time at the Ecole Normale, Paris

To get the last poems of Yeats,
You need not mug up on dates;
All a reader requires
Is some knowledge of gyres,
And the sort of people he hates.
W. H. Auden, *Academic Graffiti,* on W. B. Yeats

That old yahoo . . . His stories impressed me as being on the whole like
gruel spooned up off a dirty floor.
Jane Barlow (1857-1917) on George Moore

An insensible mass of alcohol, nicotine, and feminine intoxication. A
heap of guts. With no end for it.
Samuel Beckett (1906-1989) letter to Arland Ussher (1937), on himself

I don't give a damn for art. I'm just in it for the dough.
Brendan Behan (1923-1964), interview with Robert Robinson in the
London *Sunday Graphic* (1956)

You had to look twice to see if he was there at all.
Brendan Behan on Brian O'Nolan (1911-1966), quoted in Anthony
Cronin, *No Laughing Matter: The Life and Times of Flann O'Brien* (1989)

If any young woman finds it she should hand it to her mother without
reading it.
Dominic Behan (1928-1989) on the lost manuscript of his autobiography

We are known as the Ballygowan generation.
Dermot Bolger, commenting on the relative sobriety of contemporary
writers

. . . in an experience of sixty years this is quite the craziest piece of Irish I
have ever met.

What most surprises me is the self-assurance of its author – a man who
demonstrates twenty times on every page that he is the veriest tyro in the
Irish language. . . .   Constructions such as he writes have never before
been seen in Irish, and one earnestly hopes that nothing of the kind will
ever be repeated.

The late Stephen McKenna at one time proposed to write a book *How to Write Irish, by One Who Can't* and here, I am convinced, we have an author who could take up his project with every hope of success . . .   My advice to you is – to spend none of the firm's money on this work.
Browne & Nolan's reader's report on *An Béal Bocht* by Flann O'Brien, as quoted in Myles na Gopaleen, *The Hair of the Dogma* (1977); however it was almost wholly a confection of Myles's own. The actual reader's report was guardedly favourable.

The stupid person's idea of a clever person.
Elizabeth Bowen (1899-1973), on Aldous Huxley, in the London *Spectator,* 1936

. . . a splendid talker and a handsome man, but a voluptuary. As he walked from you, there was something in the motion of his hips and back that was disagreeable.
John Burroughs, US naturalist, on Oscar Wilde

One would never have guessed she could write her *name.*
Lord Byron, *Letters and Journals,* 1821, on Maria Edgeworth

I believe you have eaten your own heart.
Mrs Patrick Campbell, Letter to George Bernard Shaw, November 1912

That old pink petulant walrus.
Henry Channon on George Moore

. . . just a waste of everybody's time and it made me ashamed to think that such balls could be taken seriously for a moment.
Noel Coward, on *Waiting for Godot* (1960)

John Millington Synge and the priest in Inishmore did not see altogether eye to eye. When they met one Sunday:
"Did you be reading your Bible this day?"
"Well now," said John Synge. "I did not."
"Well, bedad, Mr Synge," says the Father, "if y'ever go to Heaven it's a great laugh ye'll have on us."
From Ian Dall, *Here Are Stones* (1931)

Reading AE's poems is like being inside a feather mattress.
Denis Donoghue, *We Irish* (1986)

Of all the impudent productions that have ever been intruded on the
patience of the public, we believe that none has ever yet appeared, which
if it approximated, has exceeded "The Travels of an Irish Gentleman in
Search of A Religion".
Dublin University Magazine, on Thomas Moore (April 1842)

Every man has his element: Sheridan's is hot water.
Lord Eldon, on Richard Brinsley Sheridan

I have very little estate, but what lies under the Circumference of my Hat;
and should I, by mischance, come to lose my Head, I should not be worth
a Groat.
George Farquhar (1678-1707), *The Picture,* on himself

Farquhar, the future playwright, while still a student at Trinity College,
was asked to write an exercise on 'Our Lord Walking Upon the Water'. He
failed to hand in his paper, and when asked for it, proposed to produce an
extempore instead, and offered: "He that is born to be hanged will never
be drowned."

A libel on Irish peasant men, and worst still upon Irish peasant girlhood.
Freeman's Journal, on J. M. Synge's *The Playboy of the Western World*
(January 1907)

On a train journey he overheard someone say, "That can't be Percy
French. He died last year in Naples of delirium tremens." French's com-
ment was, "As I was practically a teetotaller and had never been to Naples
I did not trouble to verify the statement."
Recorded of Percy French (1854-1920) in Vivien Igoe, *A Literary Guide to
Dublin* (1994)

Here lies Nolly G., for shortness called Noll,
Who wrote like an angel, and talked like poor Poll.
David Garrick, *Impromptu Epitaph,* on Oliver Goldsmith

She manifests a prodigious respect for something that she dignifies with the name of Nature, which, it seems, governs the world, and, as we gather from her creed, is to be honoured by libertinism in the women, disloyalty in the men and atheism in both.
William Gifford, *The Quarterly Review*, on *Ida of Athens* by Lady Morgan (Sydney Owenson)

Oliver St John Gogarty had told James Joyce that it was W. B. Yeats's fortieth birthday:
"Yeats was lodging at the Cavendish Hotel, in Rutland Square, and he solemnly walked in and knocked on Yeats's door. When Yeats opened the door of the sitting-room, he said, 'What age are you, sir?' and Yeats said, 'I'm forty.' 'You are too old for me to help. I bid you good-bye.' And Yeats was greatly impressed by the impertinence of the thing."
Oliver St John Gogarty (1878-1957), *Irish Literary Portraits*

Good acting covers a multitude of defects. It explains the success of Lady Gregory's plays.
Oliver St John Gogarty

Nothing but a long wail.
Oliver St John Gogarty, on Samuel Beckett's *Waiting for Godot*.

They persisted in the belief that poverty and savage existence on remote rocks was a most poetical way for people to be, provided they were other people.
Myles na Gopaleen (Brian O'Nolan, 1911-1966), *The Hair of the Dogma* (1977), on Synge-George Moore-Gregory-Martyn, with Yeats in the background.

. . . an ignorant affected interloper in a uniquely decent, stable and civilised community.
Myles naGopaleen, *The Hair of the Dogma*, on J. M. Synge's sojourn in the Aran Islands

A greater parcel of bosh and bunk than Flower's Islandman has rarely been imposed on the unsuspecting public.
Myles naGopaleen, *The Hair of the Dogma*, on the English version of *An t-Oileánach* by Tomás O Criomhthain

He is a literary charlatan of the extremist order. His principal book, *Ulysses*, is an anarchical production, infamous in taste, in style, in everything. He is a sort of Marquis de Sade, but does not write as well. There are no English critics of weight or judgment who consider Mr Joyce an author of any importance.
Edmund Gosse, English literary critic, on James Joyce (1924)

He rose above the depressing influences of low birth to sink under the caresses of the high-born.
Thomas Colley Grattan, *Beaten Paths and Those Who Trod Them*, on Thomas Moore

The first man to have cut a swathe through the theatre and left it strewn with virgins.
Frank Harris, on George Bernard Shaw

The author all the time seems to be on his best behaviour, as if writing a comedy was no very creditable employment.
William Hazlitt, on the plays of Sir Richard Steele

He looked as though begotten between a toad and cupid.
Theodore Hook, on George Moore

The Revd Father Meehan . . . was a friend of MacCarthy - that is until MacCarthy sent him one of his Calderón translations. The translation was immediately returned by Father Meehan accompanied by a note which said, 'The Rev Father Meehan thinks very little of Mr MacCarthy or Mr Calderón, and he has found in the *Penny Warbler* better poetry than produced by either.' Not to be outdone, MacCarthy read through some copies of the *Penny Warbler* until he came upon the line, 'A queer little man, with a very red nose,' a description which aptly fitted the Revd Meehan. He sent this to the priest with the page well marked.
Vivien Igoe, *Literary Dublin* (1994), on Denis MacCarthy (1817-1882)

It fulfils the first law of Anglo-Irish literature: it makes the native Irish appear a race of congenital idiots.
Denis Ireland, *From the Irish Shore* (1936), on Denis Johnston's *The Moon in the Yellow River*

Ulysses – a dogged attempt to cover the universe with mud.
Henry James

Lady Blessington might have gone down to posterity with a fair and
distinguished literary reputation, if she had never published her works . . .
they really possess no merit whatever . . . pervaded by bad taste and
disreputable incidents.
John Cordy Jeaffreson, *Novels and Novelists*

The most licentious of modern versifiers . . . sits down to ransack the
impure places of his memory for inflammatory images and expressions,
and commits them laboriously to writing, for the purpose of insinuating
pollution into the minds of unknown and unsuspecting readers.
Francis Jeffrey, *The Edinburgh Review* (1806), on Thomas Moore. This
review led to a duel between the two men.

The misfortune of Goldsmith in conversation is this: he goes on without
knowing how he is to get off.
Samuel Johnson, on Oliver Goldsmith

It is amazing how little Goldsmith knows. He seldom comes where he is
not more ignorant than anyone else.
Samuel Johnson, on Oliver Goldsmith. He also said: "Goldsmith's mind is
entirely unfurnished."

Such an excess of stupidity is not in nature.
Samuel Johnson on the actor Thomas Sheridan

Irresponsible braggart ... flippertygibbet pope of chaos.
Henry Arthur Jones on George Bernard Shaw

He said he thought his son Jim had had a great future as a singer and
should have pursued that career.
John Joyce, father of James Joyce, quoted in Anthony Cronin, *No
Laughing Matter: The Life and Times of Flann O'Brien* (1989)

Why don't you write books people can read?
Mrs Nora Joyce, to her husband James

It serves me right for writing something a policeman could understand.
Patrick Kavanagh (1904-1967), when visited by the police on account of
sexual references being detected in *The Great Hunger*

Don't introduce me to nonentities.
Patrick Kavanagh at a party, quoted in Bryan Macmahon, *Here's Ireland*
(1970)

The dirtiest, most indecent, most obscene thing ever written . . . My
God, what a clumsy "olla putrida" James Joyce is! Nothing but old fags
and cabbage-stumps of quotations from the Bible and the rest, stewed in
the juice of deliberate journalistic dirty-mindedness.
D. H. Lawrence, on *Ulysses*

. . . there would be no end were I to point out all the unIrish points of
Moore's poetry . . . There's the Vale of Avoca, for instance, a song upon a
Valley in Wicklow, but which would suit any other valley in the world,
provided always that it has three syllables, and the middle one of due
length.
William Maginn, *Magazine Miscellanies* (1841)

"You're not quite clever enough for us here, Oscar. Better run up to
Oxford."
J. P. Mahaffy (1839-1919), to Oscar Wilde, at Trinity College

Nothing happens, twice.
Vivian Mercier on *Waiting for Godot* (1948)

. . . an umbrella left behind at a picnic.
George Moore (1852-1933), on William Butler Yeats

Scratch a Moore, and you yourself will bleed.
Version of the family motto by George Moore

I suspect that Beckett is a confidence trick perpetrated on the twentieth
century by a theatre-hating God. He remains the only playwright in my
experience capable of making forty minutes seem like an eternity and the
wrong kind of eternity at that.
Sheridan Morley, in *Punch,* on Samuel Beckett (1973)

Shaw writes his plays for the ages: the ages between five and twelve.
George Jean Nathan

That refurbisher of skivvies' stories
Flann O'Brien (Brian O'Nolan, 1911-1966) on James Joyce, quoted in
Anthony Cronin, *No Laughing Matter: The Life and Times of Flann
O'Brien* (1989)

I think Mr Kavanagh is on the right track here. Perhaps the *Irish Times,*
timeless champion of our peasantry, will oblige us with a series in this
strain covering such rural complexities as inflamed goat-udders, warble-
pocked shorthorn, contagious abortion, non-ovoid oviducts and nervous
disorder among the gentlemen who pay the rent.
Letter from Flann O'Brien to the *Irish Times,* 1940, following publication
of Patrick Kavanagh's *Spraying the Potatoes*

Oh Eire! he was false to you, your big and artless child,
His pink and white simplicity by Sasanach defiled!
Susan Mitchell (1868-1930), *Lines on George Moore,* quoted in W. P.
Ryan, *The Pope's Green Island* (1912)

But W.B. was the boy for me – he of the dim wan clothes,
And - don't let on I said it – not above a bit of pose;
And they call his writing Literature, as everybody knows.
Susan Mitchell, Parody of George Moore, quoted in Hugh Kenner: *A
Colder Eye: The Modern Irish Writers* (1983)

You seem Mr Yeats, to be getting beautifully worse; you astonish me more
and more. There seem to be shallows in you of which no-one ever
dreamed.
Sean O'Casey (1880-1964), Letter to William Butler Yeats, May 1928

Sweet is the way of the sinner
Sad, death without God's praise
My life on you, Oscar boy,
Yourself had it both ways.
Ulick O'Connor, *Oscar Wilde,* from the Gaelic of Brendan Behan

I regard the visit as a duty to posterity.
Ezra Pound, on a proposed visit to W. B. Yeats at Thoor Ballylee, where
he would be "bored by talk on spiritualism."

Some men kiss and tell, but George Moore tells and doesn't kiss.
Sarah Purser (1848-1943) on George Moore

No author, particularly a female, should pander to those who relish filth,
and *that* means ninety-nine per cent of this rotten generation.
Amanda McKittrick Ros (1860-1939), *Donald Dudley The Bastard Critic*

Donkeyosities, egotistical earthworms, hogwashing hooligans, critic cads,
random hacks of illiteration, talent wipers of wormy ordure, the gas-bag
section, poking hounds, poisonous apes, maggotty numbskulls, evil-
minded snapshots of spleen and, worst of all, the mushroom class of idiots.
Amanda McKittrick Ros, on critics

You must not suppose, because I am a man of letters, that I have never
tried to earn an honest living.
George Bernard Shaw (1856-1950), preface to *The Irrational Knot*

I had ten years of it on the Committee of Management of the Society of
Authors, and the first lesson I learned was that when you take the field
for the authors you will be safer without a breastplate than without a
backplate.
George Bernard Shaw

In Ireland they try to make a cat clean by rubbing its nose in its own
filth. Mr Joyce has tried the same treatment on the human subject.
George Bernard Shaw, on James Joyce's *Ulysses,* 1921

Steele might become a reasonably good writer if he would pay a little
attention to grammar, learn something about the propriety and
disposition of words and incidentally, get some information on the subject
he intends to handle.
Jonathan Swift (1667-1745), on Sir Richard Steele

A silent sinner, nights and days,
No human heart to him drew nigh,

Alone he wound his wonted ways,
Alone and little loved did die.
Self-composed Epitaph of John Millington Synge (1871-1909)

Insufferable both to equals and inferiors, and unsafe for his superiors to countenance.
Jack Temple, nephew of Swift's patron Sir William Temple, on the young Jonathan Swift

A monster gibbering shrieks, and gnashing imprecations against mankind, tearing down all shreds of modesty, past all sense of manliness and shame; filthy in word, filthy in thought, furious, raging, obscene.
William Makepeace Thackeray, on Jonathan Swift

He writes fiction as if it were a painful duty.
Oscar Wilde (1854-1900), on Henry James

That vague formless obscene face.
Oscar Wilde on George Moore

In the old days books were written by men of letters and read by the public, Nowadays books are written by the public and read by nobody.
Oscar Wilde in *The Saturday Review* (1894)

He hasn't an enemy in the world; and none of his friends like him.
Oscar Wilde, on George Bernard Shaw

Now don't think I have anything against her moral character, but from the way she writes, she ought to be here.
Oscar Wilde, discussing the novelist Marie Corelli with one of the warders of Reading Gaol

The difference between journalism and literature is that journalism is unreadable and literature is unread.
Oscar Wilde

Every great man nowadays has his disciples, and it is always Judas who writes his biography.
Oscar Wilde

He wrote brilliant English until he discovered grammar.
Oscar Wilde on George Moore.

The work of a queasy undergraduate.
Virginia Woolf, on *Ulysses*

. . . whilst in many places the effect of *Ulysses* on the reader undoubtedly
is somewhat emetic, nowhere does it tend to be aphrodisiac.
US District Judge John M. Woolsey, in the obscenity hearing on James
Joyce's *Ulysses*

Not worth powder and shot.
John Butler Yeats on George Moore

When he arrived in Dublin, all the doors in Upper Ely Place had been
painted white by an agreement between the landlord and the tenants.
Moore had his door painted green, and three Miss Beams . . . who lived
next door protested to the landlord. There began a correspondence
between Moore and the landlord wherein Moore insisted on his position
as an art critic, that the whole decoration of his house required a green
door . . . the indignant young women bought a copy of *Esther Waters,* tore
it up, put the fragments into a large envelope, wrote thereon: "Too filthy
to keep in the house," dropped it into his letter-box. I was staying with
Moore. I let myself in with a latch-key some night after twelve, and found
a note on the hall-table asking me to put the door on the chain. As I was
undressing, I heard Moore trying to get in; when I opened the door and
pointed to the note, he said: "Oh, I forgot. Every night I go out at eleven,
at twelve, at one, and rattle my stick on the railing to make the Miss
Beams' dog bark."
W. B. Yeats, *Dramatis Personae, 1896-1903. Esther Waters* was the "low
life" novel that brought George Moore some notoriety.

Is this to be the ever-recurring celebration of the arrival of Irish genius?
W. B Yeats, on the riots following the opening of O'Casey's *The Plough
and the Stars* in Dublin, February 1926

Neither Christ not Buddha not Socrates wrote a book, for to do that is to
exchange life for a logical process.
W. B Yeats, *Estrangement,* from *Autobiography*

But was there ever dog that praised his fleas?
W. B. Yeats, *To a Poet, who would have me praise certain bad Poets,
Imitators of his and mine*

A face carved out of a turnip
W. B. Yeats (1865-1939), on George Moore

He is an atheist who trembles in the haunted corridor.
W. B. Yeats, Letter to Æ (George Russell), July 1921, on George Bernard
Shaw

Stop babbling, man. How much?
W. B Yeats (attributed) on being told on the telephone by Robert Smilley,
editor of the *Irish Times,* that he had won the Nobel Prize for Literature
(1923)

The way Shaw believes in himself is very refreshing, in these atheistic days
when so many people believe in no God at all.
Israel Zangwill, on George Bernard Shaw

Church and Churchmen

"You feed the poor on wealth that has been given not you, but to God;
wherefore then do you limit your giving?"
Said by the hundred-and-first poor man to St Columcille, who had set
out to feed a hundred poor men.

Although a completely non-verbal and passive form of assault, it may be
noted that fasting as a weapon has a long history in Ireland . . .
"Máelruain never fasted but thrice since he settled in Tallaght – namely
against Antry, son of Fallmuire, about a business that arose between the
monastery of Tallaght and him. After the first fasting, the king's leg broke
in two; after the second the fire fell and burnt him from top to toe; after
the third fasting the king died."
E.J. Gwynn and W.J. Purton, *The Monastery of Tallaght,* in "Proceedings
of the Royal Irish Academy", 1911, quoted in Françoise Henry, *Irish Art
in the Early Christian Period* (1947)

Look down, St Patrick, look, we pray,
On thine own Church and steeple;
Convert thy Dean, on this great day;
Or else God help the people.
Anonymous lines said to have been affixed to the door of St Patrick's
Cathedral on the installation of Jonathan Swift as Dean.

St Kevin was one day going up Derrybawn, and he met with a woman
who was carrying five loaves in her apron.
"What have you there, good woman?" asked St Kevin.
In case the holy man might ask her for bread, the woman replied, "Five
stones."
"If they are stones," said the saint, "I pray they may become loaves. But if
they are loaves, I pray they may become stones."
With that, she let them fall from her apron. And stones they were.
Traditional, from *Irish Folk Tales,* ed. Henry Glassie, 1985

Out on the road, a parish priest met one of his parishioners, a well-known drinker, and clearly the worse for wear.
"Oh, Tom," he said in a reproving tone. "Drunk again."
"Never mind, Father," replied Tom. "So I am too."
Traditional

No Pope here.
Lucky old Pope.
Belfast graffito, with additional comment

Those who gave me hard drink in the afternoon were generally bishops.
John Ardagh, *Ireland and the Irish* (1994)

"An' what is the Black Pig, Barney?"
"The Prosbytarian Church, that stretches from Enniskillen to Darry, an' back again from Darry to Enniskillen."
William Carleton (1794-1869), *The Irish Prophecy Man*

The devil who animates Protestantism does not hold himself obliged to honour any promise.
Cardinal Paul Cullen (1803-1878)

Among the best traitors that Ireland has ever had, Mother Church ranks at the very top.
Bernadette Devlin (1947-)

"By Jesus, I never would have done it but I thought the Bishop was in it."
Reply said to have been made by Garrett More Fitzgerald, "the Great Earl", to King Henry VII of England, who accused him of burning Cashel Cathedral

His fat hands twitching on the rim of the pulpit put you in mind of fish dying on the harbour wall.
Hugh Leonard (1926-), *Home Before Night*

Swift wondered how it was that every virtuous English bishop translated to Ireland was murdered on Hounslow Heath and his place taken by a highwayman, but I wondered what happened to those nice, broad-minded curates one met after they became parish priests.
Frank O'Connor (1903-1966), *My Father's Son*

Between you and me and the wall, Thomas Aquinas was a bloody old cod.
Unidentified Wicklow curate to Frank O'Connor, recorded in
My Father's Son

England and Ireland all over
I perceive to have become unwise:
They are fonder of food and women
Than of the Virgin, God or Heaven.

Their bishops and their wives in woe shall be,
Wailing their matins in bitter tears;
Foot to foot in the depths of hell,
In flames of fire face to face.
Eoghan O Dubhthaigh, translated by John O'Daly, *The Apostasy of Myles
Magreth, Archbishop of Cashel* (17th century)

An Irish atheist is a man who wishes to God that he could believe in God.
J. P. Mahaffy (1839-1919)

"Patrick," says Ossian, "for what did God damn all that of people?"
"For eating the apple of commandment," says Saint Patrick.
"If I had known that your God was so narrow-sighted that he damned all
that of people for one apple, we would have sent three horses and a mule
carrying apples to God's heaven for him."
Douglas Hyde (1860-1949), *Ossian of the Flail,* from Gaelic

"A true Irish bishop," said Archbishop Bolton, "has nothing more to do
than to eat, drink, grow fat, rich, and die."
W.E.H. Lecky, *Ireland in the Eighteenth Century* (1902), on Church of
Ireland bishops

Heaven may be for the laity, but this world is certainly for the clergy.
George Moore (1852-1933)

The religion at present authorised by the priests is the Catholic religion
. . . without priests no religion can be considered seriously. It has no
backbone and no terror.
Liam O'Flaherty, *Tourists' Guide to Ireland* (1930)

The religion and the Pope give us Catholicism; most priests give us
nothing but Parochialism.
'Pat' (I.P.D. Kenny) *Economics for Irishmen* (1906)

The Roman Catholic Church is getting nearer to Communism every day.
Rev Ian Paisley, quoted in the *Irish Times,* September 1969

Socialists are a Protestant variety of Communists
Priest in Dingle, June 1969, quoted in Conor Cruise O'Brien, *States of Ireland*

Laurence Sterne, clergyman and author of *Tristram Shandy,* once entered a coffee house at York in England, and was introduced to a man who remarked: "I detest parsons."
"Indeed, sir," said Sterne, "so does my dog. No sooner have I put on my gown and cassock, than he falls to yapping and barking."
"How long has he done this?" asked a bystander.
"Ever since he was a *puppy*, sir," said Sterne, giving the parson-hater a meaningful look.

The emancipated and liberal Irishman, like the emancipated and liberal Frenchman, may go to Mass, may tell his beads, or sprinkle his mistress with holy water, but neither the one nor the other will attend to the rusty and extinguished thunderbolts of the Vatican or the idle anathemas which, indeed, His Holiness is now-a-days too prudent and cautious to issue.
Theobald Wolfe Tone (1763-1798), *An Argument on Behalf of the Catholics of Ireland*

Archbishop Whateley, as head of the Church of Ireland, had an aide de camp attached to his household. The young soldier, hoping to impress the Archbishop with his wit, one day asked him if he knew the difference between a donkey and a Catholic priest.
"No," said Whateley, "what is it?"
"Well, sir, a donkey has a cross upon his back, and a Catholic priest has a cross upon his front."
"Tell me," said Whateley, "do you know the difference between an aide de camp and an ass?"
"No, sir."
"Neither do I," said the Archbishop.
Richard Whateley (1787-1863) was Archbishop of Dublin and a supporter of Catholic emancipation

Clothes and Fashions

"Will yez look at the Irishers trying to look like stained-glass windows?"
Dublin fishmongers commenting on ladies in "Celtic" costume, quoted in
Mary Colum, *Life and the Dream* (1928)

The trowser is a long stock of frieze, close to his thighs, and drawn on
almost to his waist, but very scant, and the pride of it is to wear it so in
suspense that the beholder may suspect it to be falling from his arse.
Luke Gernon, *A Discourse of Ireland* (1620)

. . . how are the second-hand breeks?
– They fit well enough, Stephen answered.
Buck Mulligan attacked the hollow beneath his underlip.
– The mockery of it, he said contentedly, second leg they should be. God
knows what poxy bowsy left them off.
James Joyce (1882-1941), *Ulysses*

. . . an occasional fellow without any breeches on him but wearing a
lady's underskirt instead. It was stated that he as such wore Gaelic
costume. . . There were men present wearing a simple, unornamented
dress – these, I thought, had little Gaelic; others had such nobility, style
and elegance in their feminine attire that it was evident that their Gaelic
was fluent.
Flann O'Brien (Brian O'Nolan, 1911-1966), *The Poor Mouth*, translated
by Patrick C. Power

Don't buy British blazers.
Schoolboy graffito by Brian O'Nolan, referring to the Blackrock College
uniform, and said to be Flann O'Brien's "first published sentence".

Twenty years ago the trouser pockets of the cheapest suits were made of
canvas, and were still intact long after the suit had wasted away. All
pockets of today are made apparently from cheap Egyptian cotton. It is
my submission that human beings are entitled to pockets not inferior in

quality to those of a snooker table.
Myles na Gopaleen (Brian O'Nolan), *The Hair of the Dogma*

The poor people go totally naked, although the majority wear those cloaks, good or bad. . . the queen was barefoot, and her handmaidens, twenty in number, were dressed as I have told you above with their shameful parts showing. And you should know that all these people were no more ashamed of this than of showing their faces.
Ramon de Perelós, *Voyage to St Patrick's Purgatory*, late 14th century

. . . one of civilization's greatest botches.
J. D. Sheridan, *While the Humour Is On Me* (1954), referring to cuff-links

Fashion is a form of ugliness so intolerable that we have to alter it every six months.
Oscar Wilde (1854-1900)

Curses

The curse of Cromwell on it.
Traditional

May the curse of Mary Malone and her nine blind illegitimate children chase you so far over the hills of Damnation that the Lord himself won't find you with a telescope.
Traditional

May you melt off the earth like snow off the ditch.
Traditional

Bruadar and Smith and Glinn,
Amen, dear God, I pray,
May they lie low in waves of woe
And tortures slow each day . . .

Blindness come down on Smith,
Palsy on Bruadar come,
Amen, O King of Brightness! Smite
Glinn in his members numb.
From a 26-verse Gaelic curse (17th century), translated by Douglas Hyde in *Religious Songs of Connacht*

He that won't drink this, whether he be priest, bishop, deacon, bellows-blower, gravedigger, or any other of the fraternity of the clergy, may a north wind blow him to the south, and a west wind blow him to the east! May he have a dark night, a lee shore, a rank storm, and a leaky vessel to carry him over the River Styx. May the dog Cerberus make a meal of his rump and Pluto a snuffbox of his skull! May the devil jump down his throat with a red-hot harrow, and with every pin tear out a gut, and blow him with a clean carcase to hell! Amen!
From a Williamite toast of the 1690s

They won't put him in the pit,
Says the Shan Van Vocht,
Where the common sinners sit,
Says the Shan Van Vocht,
But he'll get a warrum sate
Up beside the special grate
Where his father bakes in state
Says the Shan Van Vocht.
Anonymous 19th-century song on the death of George Beresford, an
evicting landlord

There are three watching for my death, the Devil, the Children, and the
Worms; the Worms that would rather have my body than my soul and my
wealth; the Children that would rather have my wealth than that my soul
should be at one with my body; the Devil that has no desire for the
wealth of the world, nor for my body, but only my soul. Christ that was
crucified on the tree, let the Worms, the Devil and the Children be
hanged by a ged.
Anonymous curse, quoted in Padraic Colum (1881-1972), *My Irish Year*

Punish the slave driver, bell him, exhibit him,
Show him around for a while ere you gibbet him;
Pitchcap and thumbscrew and maul him and mangle him,
Torture him, tar him, and finally strangle him.
Anonymous, strikers' broadsheet of the 1930s

Vladimir: Morpion.
Estragon: Sewer rat.
Vladimir: Curate.
Estragon: Cretin.
Vladimir: Crrritic!
Samuel Beckett (1906-1989), *Waiting for Godot*

Some day if God's in Heaven,
Overlooking his Preserve,
I know the men that shot him down
Will get what they deserve.
Tribute placed in *Belfast Telegraph,* September 1986, for UVF member
John Bingham

It's a salt herring you ought to have tied to your tail, an' be turned out before a drag-hunt, you skulkin' vagabone.
William Carleton (1798-1869), *Mysterious Doings at Slathbeg*

"God of justice," I sighed, "send your spirit down
On these lords so cruel and so proud,
And soften their hearts and relax their frown,
Or else," I cried aloud –
"Vouchsafe thy strength to the peasant's hand
To drive them at length from off the land."
Thomas Davis (1815-1845), *A Scene in the South*

May every buck flea from here to Bray
Jump through the bed he lies on,
And by some mistake may he shortly take
A flowing pint of poison
Popular versified curse, quoted by Hugh Kenner, *A Colder Eye: Modern Irish Writers* (1983)

May hound-wounding, heart-ache, and vultures gouging her eyes,
Derangement and madness on her mind come soon!
May the entrails and mansion of pleasure of this worm fall out!
But may she still be alive till everyone is sick of the sight.
Peadar O'Doirin, *An Guairne*

It was wonderful the way the saints cud curse in the oul' days. The same Patrick was at it by all accounts. He'd ring he's Bell on ye and curse ye for little. And ride over ye if he took the notion.
T. F. Paterson, Armagh historian, quoted in Oswell Blakeston, *Thank You, Now* (1960)

Weary men, what reap ye? Golden corn for the stranger.
What sow ye? Human corses that wait for the avenger.
Fainting forms, hunger-stricken, what see you in the offing?
Stately ships to bear our food away, for the strangers' scoffing.
"Speranza" (Jane Elgee, later Lady Wilde, 1826-1896), *The Stricken Land* (1847)

May the devil grip the whey-faced slut by the hair,
And beat bad manners out of her skin for a year.
. . . May she marry a ghost and bear him a kitten, and may
The High King of Glory permit her to get the mange.
James Stephens (1882-1950), *A Glass of Beer* (from the Gaelic of David
O'Bruadair)

Lord, confound this surly sister,
Blight her brow with blotch and blister,
Cramp her larynx, lung and liver,
In her guts a galling give her.
Let her live to earn her dinners
In Mountjoy with seedy sinners;
Lord, this judgment quickly bring,
And I'm your servant, J. M. Synge.
J.M. Synge (1871-1909), *The Curse* (To a sister of an enemy of the
playwright's who disapproved of *The Playboy*)

. . . two Aranmore men . . . were cutting and clearing bracken off an
upland farm in Fifeshire. Their store of provisions was running short, so
they made their way to the farmer for whom they were working and asked
for cheese. He pressed his own, it seems. He refused their request. "Very
well," said the older of the two, *"Bas s'—ga lá gaoithe ar bhárr ph'ce!'"*They
left. The next morning the lady of the house sent for them. "Here,"she
said, "take all the cheese you want. My Willie died last night in his bed. I
was gettin' fed up with him anyway . . . Could you teach me that curse?"
Paddy Tunney, *Where Songs Do Thunder* (1991)

Dublin and Dubliners

The glory of ould Ireland and a thousand buccaneers,
And a terror to Creation are the Dublin Fusiliers.
Quoted in Brendan Behan (1923-1964), *Confessions of an Irish Rebel*

"Come here," said I, "you skinny-looking hun bastard. I've only one hand
but I've two plates of meat and I swear if I don't break you with that one
hand for a beginning, I'll give you a kick up the balls that you won't be
forgetting, not this day or tomorrow."
What we call in the slums at home "a Ringsend uppercut . . ."
Brendan Behan, *Confessions of an Irish Rebel* (1965)

Dublin is intolerance by the sea.
Brian Behan (1927-), interviewed in London *Sunday Times,* 18th
September 1988

. . . the grey deadness and stultifying inertia of Dublin suburban living
Christy Brown (1932-1981) letter to Patricia Sheehan, September 1977

Mr James Duffy lived in Chapelizod because he wished to live as far as
possible from the city of which he was a citizen and because he found all
the other suburbs of Dublin mean, modern, and pretentious.
James Joyce (1882-1941), *A Painful Case,* from *Dubliners*

You'll always find the fashionable jackeen in Dublin.
Myles na Gopaleen (Brian O'Nolan, 1911-1966) *The Hard Life*

The Gaelic Babylon
Myles na Gopaleen, *The Hair of the Dogma*

Strumpet city in the sunset
Wilful city of savage dreamers,
So old, so sick with memories
Denis Johnston (1901-1984), *The Old Lady Says No*

Corporation houses went up, none with a bathroom, for officialdom held that a combination of cleanliness and Irishness was somehow unnatural.
Hugh Leonard (1926-), *Home before Night*

The trees along the Dodder are more sinned against than sinning.
James Montgomery. The banks of the Dodder had a name for being a lovers' lane.

Dublin is like that. We knew his local pub but not his house.
Edna O'Brien (1932-), *The Country Girl*

This is a terrible country for sexual obsession . . . I give you five cities – Tyre, Sidon, Gomorrah, Sodom and Dublin.
Flann O'Brien (Brian O'Nolan, 1911-1966), *The Dalkey Archive*

Rotten Dublin; lousy Dublin, what had it for anyone? What had it for him?
Poverty and pain and penance. These were its three castles.
Sean O'Casey (1880-1964), quoted in Garry O'Connor, *Sean O'Casey: A Life* (1988)

A long, lurching row of discontented incurables, smirched with the age-long marks of ague, fever, cancer and consumption, the soured tears of little children, and the sighs of disappointed newly-married girls.
Sean O'Casey, on the houses of Mountjoy Square, 1920

He'd . . . settled into a life of Guinness, sarcasm and late late nights, the kind of life that American academics think real Dubliners lead.
Joseph O'Connor, *Cowboys and Indians* (1991)

An August Sunday afternoon in the north side of Dublin. Epitome of all that is hot, arid, and empty.
E. O. Somerville (1855-1949) and Violet Martin Ross (1862-1915), *The Real Charlotte*

This is worse than to be back off the quay of the Blasket waiting for a calm moment to run in.
Maurice O'Sullivan, *Twenty Years A-Growing,* translated by Moya Llewelyn Davies and George Thomson, on the traffic in O'Connell Street, *c* 1930

I ever feared the tattle of this nasty town.
Jonathan Swift (1667-1745), letter to Vanessa, quoted in Victoria
Glendinning, *Jonathan Swift* (1998)

Great Insulters: Jonathan Swift

Jonathan Swift, Dean of St Patrick's, Dublin, who lived from 1667 to 1745, was a man for whom individual human targets, though attractive on occasion, were altogether too paltry. Swift's principal and gigantic target was the entire human species. He considered it stupid ("the bulk of mankind is as well qualified for flying as for thinking"), dirty, immoral and vicious. He coined the word "Yahoo," which remains current to describe a particularly unappealing person; he meant it for everyone. It comes from the fourth book of *Gulliver's Travels;* even in the first book, the King of Lilliput describes humans – admittedly as exemplified by the English – as 'the most pernicious race of odious little vermin that Nature ever suffered to crawl upon the surface of the earth.'

On several occasions Swift walked from London to Chester, and on one of these excursions he sheltered from a thunderstorm, under an oak-tree, where he was joined by a man and an extremely pregnant woman. Discovering they were on their way to be married, he offered to perform the ceremony on the spot, and they gratefully accepted. Having performed the rite, Swift then wrote out a certificate for the groom, which went thus:
"Under an oak, in stormy weather,
I joined this rogue and whore together;
And none but He who rules the thunder,
Can part this rogue and whore asunder."

Swift took a vigorous part in English politics and did not spare his opponents. Although he is remembered in Ireland as a defender of Irish liberties and of the Irish poor, he in fact disliked the country and the people intensely and longed to be back in London. But his celebrated "Modest Proposal" on behalf of the starving Irish was a shaft aimed not at them but at the uncaring Whig government in London: "a young healthy child, well-nursed, is, at a year old, a most delicious, nourishing, and wholesome food, whether stewed, roasted, boiled or baked; and I make no doubt that it will equally serve in a fricassee or a ragout. . . The skin will

make admirable gloves for ladies . . ."
When shown the motto taken by William of Orange when he became
King of England - 'Non rapui sed recepi' ('I did not take, but I was
given,' i.e. the crown), Swift observed 'The receiver's as bad as the thief.'

Swift was capable of fine, if stinging, wit, as in this verse from *On Poetry:*
'So, naturalists observe, a flea
Hath smaller fleas that on him prey;
And these have smaller fleas to bite 'em,
And so proceed ad infinitum.
Thus every poet, in his kind,
Is bit by him that comes behind.'

Moving as he did between Ireland and England, he made many
observations on the latter country, including "Burn everything that comes
from England, except the coal" (though he claimed to be quoting the late
Archbishop of Tuam). He summed up the English method of colonising
in *Gulliver's Travels* as follows: "A crew of pirates are driven by a storm
they know not whither; at length a boy discovers land from the topmast;
they go on shore to rob and plunder; they see a harmless people, are
entertained with kindness; they give the country a new name; they take
formal possession of it for their king; they set up a rotten plank or a stone
for a memorial; they murder two or three dozen natives; bring away a
couple more by force for a sample; return home and get their pardon.
Here commences a new dominion acquired with a title by divine right.
Ships are sent with the first opportunity; the natives driven out or
destroyed; their princes tortured to discover their gold; a free licence
given to all acts of inhumanity and lust, the earth reeking with the blood
of its inhabitants; and this execrable crew of butchers, employed in so
pious an expedition, is a modern colony, sent to convert and civilize an
idolatrous and barbarous people."

Swift's insults were not always satirical. One Dublin hostess went to great
trouble to arrange a splendid dinner party for him (Swift hated undue
show) and then began to apologise to him for its supposed inadequacy.
"Pox take you for a bitch," said the Dean, "why did you not get a better?
Sure, you had time enough! But since you say it is so bad, I'll e'en go
home and eat a herring."
And off he went.

So fierce a spirit could not fail to make enemies, and Swift collected many barbs. Even nine years after his death, Lady Mary Wortley Montague could write: "His character seems to me a parallel with that of Caligula, and had he had the same power, would have made the same use of it" (letter to Lady Bute, June 1754); eleven years later, Horace Walpole wrote of him to George Montague: "That brute, who hated everybody that he hoped would get him a mitre, and did not."

Family Life

Never throw stones at your mother,
You'll be sorry for it when she's dead.
Never throw stones at your mother –
Throw bricks at your father instead.
Traditional

The hound
Could never be called refined,
So push the tip of his nose
Up the Master's behind.
The Master
May alter his scholarly airs
If you stick the tip of his nose
Up the lackey's arse.
The lackey
Will rise in life
If you stuff his nose in turn
In the rear of the Master's wife.
The wife –
Who is always sniffing around –
May sniff for the rest of her days,
Nose under the tail of the hound.
Anonymous, 11th century, 'The Angry Poet of Clonmacnois', from a
translation by Frank O'Connor, *The Little Monasteries* (1963)

Woe be on marriage! It's a pity it ever existed. A person tied up in its
shelter has difficulty in getting free of it. It's a shame that whoever isn't
pleased with his wife doesn't just come out to drive her to the fair as he
would sell a cow or a sheep.
Connacht song, translated from Gaelic, quoted in T.F. O'Rahilly in
Gadelica, i (1912-13)

There was a man going to be hanged in Galway one time and his wife went to see him the night before, and all she said was, "Where will I sow the flax this year?" He was vexed at that and he said, "Is that all you are come to say to me?" "Is it that you are in a sulk because you are going to be hanged in the morning?" says the wife. That was all she said.
Traditional, from Lady Gregory, *The Kiltartan History Book*

Children were pretty things at three years old; but began to be great plagues at six, and were quite intolerable at ten.
Maria Edgeworth (1767-1849), *The Grateful Negro*

When the blind lead the blind, they both fall into – matrimony.
George Farquhar (1678-1707)

I don't think matrimony consistent with the liberty of the subject.
George Farquhar

a vast malevolent old woman . . . her girth almost exceeded her stature, and her prodigious appetite amazed me, for her cooking verged on the poisonous.
Hugh Leonard (1926-), *Home before Night,* on his grandmother

Down with marriage! It's out of date;
It exhausts the stock and cripples the state.
Bryan Merryman (1747-1805), *The Midnight Court,* translated from Gaelic by Frank O' Connor

If there were no husbands, who would look after our mistresses?
George Moore (1852-1933)

Marriage is popular because it combines the maximum of temptation with the maximum of opportunity.
George Bernard Shaw (1856-1950)

Marriage is all very well, but it isn't romance: there's nothing wrong in it.
George Bernard Shaw

There may be some doubt as to who are the best people to be in charge of children, but there can be no doubt that parents are the worst.
George Bernard Shaw

In marriage, three is company and two none.
Oscar Wilde (1854-1900), *The Importance of Being Earnest*

Relations are simply a tedious pack of people who haven't got the remotest knowledge of how to live nor the smallest instinct about when to die.
Oscar Wilde

Children begin by loving their parents. After a time, they judge them. Rarely, if ever, do they forgive them.
Oscar Wilde

Glossary of Insulting Terms

blootered: drunk

blow-in: stranger come to live in the country

bollix: silly person

caffler: fool

country cauboons: bumpkins

culchie: rustic

cute hoor: crafty, untrustworthy person on the make, especially in, or
aspiring to, politics

Fecky the Ninth: complete nitwit

gee-bag: useless person

gobdaw: drivelling idiot

gobshite: even more drivelling idiot

Jackeen: person with an inflated view of his own value, Dubliner

jibber: someone who's afraid to have a go

kilties' garters: bacon cuttings

Mary Hick: dowdy woman

old bags: middle-aged person

old pelters: decrepit old bags

Prod: a Protestant, or member of that community

sleveen: crafty female

spalpeen: rascal (originally a temporary worker who helped with the
harvest)

sparra fart: undersized person

taig: a native Irish person, and, by extension, a Catholic, from Gaelic
tadhg, poet

wee get: annoying small person or child

ya hoor: (said to a male), you fool.

Internecine Insults

From the Ferocious O'Flaherties, good Lord deliver us.
16th-century inscription from Galway city gate.

Nits make lice.
A 17th-century comment on the murder of Catholic children.

The domestic enemy.
A standard reference to the Irish people in the proceedings of the 18th century Dublin Parliament.

Fighting like divils for conciliation,
An' hatin' each other for the love of God.
Anonymous Dublin street singer (1826), words sometimes attributed to Charles Lever (1806-1872)

And when their babies learn to talk
They shout 'discrimination',
Their dad just lies in bed all day
And lives upon the nation.
Loyalist ballad of the 1950s

He took the soup.
Insult from the time of the Great Hunger (1848-52), referring to Catholics who adopted Protestantism in order to qualify for free food distribution.

They are the most displeasing people God ever made, unless it might be the ancient Jews.
Traditional, from Lady Gregory, *The Kiltartan History Book*

They might eat them.
Reply from a Royal Ulster Constabulary man to the suggestion from Scotland Yard that police horses be used in Belfast street policing

Ye never heard of the Twelfth? Away home, man, and read your Bible.
Anonymous Orangeman, when asked by a stranger about the origins of
the 12th of July parades, quoted by Meic Stephens in *Collins' Dictionary
of Literary Quotations,* from the Diary of Lady Spender (1921)

Anyone who isn't confused here doesn't really understand what's going on.
Anonymous, Belfast

Poor Paddy, of all Christian men I think
On basest food pours down the vilest drink.
William Allingham (1824-1889), *Lawrence Bloomfield*

History of Ireland – lawlessness and turbulence, robbery and oppression,
hatred and revenge, blind selfishness everywhere – no principle, no
heroism. What can be done with it?
William Allingham, *A Diary*

It is suicide to be abroad. But what is it to be at home, Mr Tyler, what is
it to be at home? A lingering dissolution.
Samuel Beckett (1906-1989), *All That Fall*

I prefer France at war to Ireland at peace.
Samuel Beckett, at the outbreak of the Second World War

. . . the headmaster entreated Beckett to take his teaching more seriously
for he had been entrusted with the education of young men who were
"the cream of Ulster."
"Yes, I know," Beckett replied dryly, "all rich and thick."
Deirdre Bair, *Samuel Beckett* (1978)

Pat: He was an Anglo-Irishman.
Meg: In the blessed name of God, what's that?
Pat: A Protestant with a horse.
Brendan Behan (1923-1964), *The Hostage*

"I can always tell a Fenian," she said . . .
"How?" I asked.
"By their wee button noses."
Brendan Behan, *Confessions of an Irish Rebel*

The Irish charm is rather facile and also we have a tendency to say sometimes, not what we believe but what we think we are wanted to believe.
Brendan Behan, *Confessions of an Irish Rebel*

O the praties they were small, over there,
O the praties they were small, over there;
O the praties they were small, but we ate them, skin and all:
They were better than fugh-all, over there.
Quoted in Brendan Behan, *Confessions of an Irish Rebel*

Where would the Irish be without someone to be Irish at?
Elizabeth Bowen (1899-1973), *The House in Paris*

They're deserving of nothing but the government they have, and may they
long have such to rule over them.
Padraic Colum (1881-1972), *The Road Round Ireland* (1926)

Jesus must have been an Irishman. After all, He was unmarried, 32 years
old, lived at home, and His mother thought He was God.
Shane Connaughton, *Divisions of the Oscar*

Rank nurse of nonsense, on whose thankless coast
The base weed thrives, the nobler bloom is lost;
Parent of pride and poverty, where dwell
Dullness and brogue and calumny: – farewell!
Thomas Dermody, *Farewell to Ireland*

Population three million; exports, emigrants.
Percy French (1854-1920), *The First Lord Lieutenant*

When he (St Patrick) visited Ireland, there was no word in the Irish
language to express sobriety.
Oliver St John Gogarty (1878-1957), Speech in the Senate

It is the national pastime to brood full of black bile.
Oliver St John Gogarty, *As I Was Going Down Sackville Street*

The Irish people do not gladly suffer common sense.
Oliver St John Gogarty

History is more backward in Ireland than in any other country.
Alice Stopford Green, quoted in R. F. Foster, *Paddy and Mr Punch* (1993)

Of the "wee six" I sing,
Where to be saved you only must save face,
And whatever you say, you say nothing.
Seamus Heaney (1939-), *Whatever You Say, Say Nothing,* from *North*

Kelt, Briton, Roman, Saxon, Dane and Scot:
time and this island tied a crazy knot.
John Hewitt (1907-1987), *Ulsterman*

The tragedy of Northern Ireland is that it is now a society in which the
dead console the living.
Jack Holland (1947-), *New York Times Magazine,* July 1979

O Ireland, my first and only love,
Where Christ and Caesar are hand and glove!
James Joyce (1882-1941), *Gas from a Burner*

This lovely land that always sent
Her writers and artists to banishment,
And in a spirit of Irish fun
Betrayed her own leaders, one by one.
James Joyce

The old sow that eats her own farrow.
James Joyce, on Ireland, in *A Portrait of the Artist as a Young Man*

The twelfth of July, the voice of Ulster speaking,
Tart as week-old buttermilk from a churn
Patrick Kavanagh (1904-1967), *The Twelfth of July*

From Cavan and from Leitrim and from Mayo,
From all the thin-faced parishes where hills
Are perished noses running peaty water
Patrick Kavanagh, *Lough Derg*

You pratey-snapping reject of a mermaid's litter
John B. Keane, *Owl Sandwiches* (1985)

What is an Irishman but a mere machine for converting potatoes into human nature?
Edward Kenealy (1819-1880) quoted in D. J. Donoghue, *The Humour of Ireland* (1898). But he lifted the phrase from the English humorist Sydney Smith.

The more I examine Irish public utterances of all kinds, the more I find them due to mere impulse rather than orderly thought.
'Pat' (I.P.D. Kenny) *Economics for Irishmen* (1906)

Orange-ism consists mainly of a settled hallucination, and an annual brainstorm.
Tom Kettle, quoted in Ulick O'Connor, *Oliver St John Gogarty* (1964)

. . . Southward from Fatima Mansions
into the foothills
to where the transplanted can trudge
From Cherryfield Heights via Woodbine Crescent
through Bridget's Terrace and Kennedy's Villas
by Ard na Gréine and Cœl na Gaoithe
to Shangri-La for a bottle of milk;
Northward past our twinned experimental
concrete piss-towers for the underprivileged
Thomas Kinsella (1928-), *A Fond Embrace*

The Irish carry from their mother's womb not so much a fanatic heart as a begrudging one.
Professor Jo Lee, quoted in John Ardagh, *Ireland and the Irish* (1994)

A country full of genius, but with absolutely no talent.
Hugh Leonard (1926-), interviewed in the London *Times*, August 1977. This comment was also made by Micheál MacLiammoir in *Ceo Meala Lá Seaca*.

A banana republic without even the climate to grow bananas.
Hugh Leonard, *The Unimportance of Being Irish,* in *Irishmen in a Changing Society* (1986)

Between you and me and the man in the moon, there's not much worth talking about south of the Boyne.
'Nationalist Ulsterman', quoted by Robert Lynd in *Home Life in Ireland* (1909)

Everyone who is black-haired, who is a tattler, guileful, tale-bearing, noisy, contemptible, every wretched, mean, strolling, unsteady, harsh and inhospitable person, every slave, every mean thief, every churl, everybody who does not listen to music or entertainment, the disturbers of every council and every assembly, and the promoters of discord among people, these are the descendants of the Firbolg.
MacFirbis, 17th century, quoted in Sean O'Faolain, *An Irish Journey* (1940)

There were moments of despair when one could see nothing of her but poverty and ignorance and cant, the famished mouth and stubbly chin, the mackintosh limp with rain, the greasy comb and broken rosary among the litter in the pocket, the blue eyes sodden with drink, dribbling with laughter.
Micheál MacLiammoir (1899-1978), *All for Hecuba* (referring to Ireland)

Ireland. The Irish. Pigs, priests, potatoes, piety, porter.
Bryan Macmahon, *Here's Ireland* (1970)

The land of scholars and saints:
Scholars and saints my eye, the land of ambush,
Purblind manifestoes, never-ending complaints,
The born martyr and the gallant ninny
Louis MacNeice (1907-1963), *Autumn Journal*

She is both a bore and a bitch;
Better close the horizon . . .
And she gives her children neither sense nor money
Who slouch around the world with a gesture and a brogue

And a faggot of useless memories.
Louis MacNeice, *Autumn Journal*

I hate your grandiose airs,
Your sob stuff, your laugh and swagger,
Your assumption that everyone cares
Who is king of your castle.
Louis MacNeice, *Ireland, My Ireland*

God of the Irish Protestant,
Lord of our proud Ascendancy,
Soon there'll be none of us extant;
We want a few plain words with Thee.
Thou know'st our hearts are always set
On what we get, on what we get.
Susan Mitchell (1868-1930), Parody of Rudyard Kipling's *Recessional*

In Ireland the inevitable never happens, and the unexpected occurs
constantly.
J. P. Mahaffy (1839-1919)

Both Northern Ireland and the Irish Free State owe their origin not to the
force of argument but to the argument of force.
T. W. Moody, 1967, quoted in John Darby, *Conflict in Northern Ireland*
(1977)

In Ireland there is so little sense of compromise that a girl has to choose
between perpetual adoration and perpetual pregnancy.
George Moore (1852-1933)

Nothing in Ireland lasts long except the miles.
George Moore, *Ave*

"Why, you potato-faced pippin-sneezer, when did a Madagascar monkey
like you pick enough of common Christian decency to hide your Kerry
accent?"
Mrs Biddy Moriarty, Dublin stall-holder, to Daniel O'Connell, quoted in
D. J. Donoghue, *The Humour of Ireland* (1898)

You are Irish you say lightly, and allocated to you are the tendencies to be wild, wanton, drunk, superstitious, unreliable, backward, toadying and prone to fits.
Edna O'Brien (1932-), *Mother Ireland*

Obtuseness and a very fine conceit of herself have always been characteristics of the Old Lady, as indeed of her noblest servants.
Kate O'Brien (1897-1974), *My Ireland*

We've spread ourselves over the world, and left our own sweet land thin.
Sean O'Casey (1880-1964)

The Irish man never grows up: he keeps not only the little boy alive in him, and the anarchic spirit, but the basic fear. Comically engaging in his infantilism, he is tragically inadequate when facing reality.
Garry O'Connor, *Sean O'Casey: A Life* (1988)

An Irish queer is a fellow who prefers women to drink.
Sean O'Faolain (1900-1991)

. . . snoring gently behind the Green Curtain that we have been rigging up for the last thirty years – Thought-proof, World-proof, Life-proof.
Sean O'Faolain, on Ireland in 1951

Are You Irish or Normal?
Sean O'Grada, book title (1984)

Our ancestors cut a civilisation out of the bogs and meadows of this country while Mr Haughey's ancestors were wearing pig-skins and living in caves.
Rev. Ian Paisley, speech at Omagh, 1981

Great my shame:
My own children that sold their mother.
Patrick Pearse (1879-1916)

Put an Irishman on the spit and you can always get another Irishman to turn him.
George Bernard Shaw (1856-1950)

She spoke calmly and purposefully. "During the war my husband made bombs. He spent four years making bombs. I wish to Jaysus I had one of them now."
Patrick Shea, quoted in Jonathan Bardon, *A History of Ulster* (1992), on a Belfast widow refused unemployment benefit

I had very good hawks and hounds but we have not had more success in any sport than Tory-hunting. The gentlemen of the country have been so hearty in that chase that of thirteen in the county where I live in November, the last was killed two days before I left home.
Sir William Stewart, of Newtownstewart, Letter to the Duke of Ormond, March 1683. A Tory was a landless Catholic outlaw

A servile race in folly nursed,
Who truckle most when treated worst.
Jonathan Swift (1667-1745)

He gave the little wealth he had
To build a house for fools and mad,
And showed, by one satiric touch,
No nation wanted it so much.
Jonathan Swift, on his bequest to found St Patrick's Hospital

We Irish are too poetical to be poets: we are a nation of brilliant failures
Oscar Wilde (1854-1900); he added, "But we are the greatest talkers since the Greeks."

Was it for this the wild geese spread
The grey wing upon every tide?
Romantic Ireland's dead and gone,
It's with O'Leary in the grave.
W. B. Yeats (1865-1939), *September 1913*

Great Insulters: Richard Brinsley Sheridan

The Dublin-born Sheridan (1751-1816) is best remembered as the witty playwright of *The Rivals,* but in his own lifetime was far more engaged in politics and the business of the theatre than he was in writing. He spent his working life in London, although he did not forget his Irish origins. In 1780 he was elected MP for Stafford and generally supported the Whigs, though in a somewhat independent manner.

Some of his best sayings come from the House of Commons. In one debate on Ireland, when a previous speaker had recommended firm and harsh laws to keep the Irish under submission, and pointed out that there could be no possibility of strife when there was no possibility of opposition being offered, Sheridan rose to point out, silkily, that the same was true of rape. Of Henry Dundas, the Tory "dictator" of Scotland, he observed that, "the Honourable gentleman gets his jests from his memory, and his facts from his imagination."

Perhaps his greatest moment was in the trial of Warren Hastings, administrator of British India. He railed against Hastings in many speeches. "His crimes are the only great thing about him, and they are contrasted by the littleness of his motives," he said in one of them.

Sheridan enjoyed the social life of the English capital. On one occasion he encountered two royal dukes in St James's, then as now the clubland of the wealthy.
'I say, Sherry," said one, 'we were just wondering whether you were more of a fool than a rogue. What d'ye say?'
Sheridan inserted himself between them and took each by the arm.
'I'd say I was in between the two,' he replied.

Sheridan's son, Tom, possessed some of his father's wit. But he was outdone on the occasion when he said to his father, "When I get into Parliament, I will pledge myself to no party, but write upon my forehead in legible characters 'To Be Let.'" Sheridan responded: "And under it,

Tom, write 'Unfurnished'."

Although it is no aim of this collection to report compliments, Sheridan, displaying the other side of the coin of wit, surely made one of the finest compliments ever when he invited a young lady into the garden. "I would like my roses to see you," he said.

Ireland and The Irish, as Seen by Others

The Irish don't know what they want and won't be happy until they get it.
British graffito

In an 18th-century London coffee-house, a man sat writing a letter, when
he became aware of someone peering over his shoulder at what he was
writing. Something about the observer suggested he was an Irishman, and
writer brought his letter to an end by writing, "I would say more but an
impudent Irish fellow is looking over my shoulder."
"You lie, you scoundrel!" cried the Irishman.
From *Remarkable Sayings of the English Nation* (1801)

When the Irishman Richard Harris was named Best Actor at Cannes, the
London press rejoiced, "British actor wins award"; when he got drunk a
month later, the headlines ran, "Irish actor arrested in bar."
John Ardagh, *Ireland and the Irish* (1994)

I sometimes wish we could submerge the whole lot of them and their
island for say, ten years, under the waves of the Atlantic.
H. H. Asquith, British Prime Minister, diary entry, September 1914

Now Ireland has her madness and her weather still
For poetry makes nothing happen.
W.H. Auden, *In Memory of W.B. Yeats*

A nation of brilliant failures.
Max Beerbohm. Beerbohm appears to have lifted this from Oscar Wilde.
See Internecine Insults.

What barbarous habits these Irish have in all their modes of life, and how
far they are removed from anything like civilisation!
English lady in William Carleton's *The Connaught Pig-Driver*

Human swinery has reached its *acme*.
Thomas Carlyle, *Reminiscences of My Irish Journey in 1849,* on Westport
workhouse, during the Great Hunger

Ireland is like a half-starved rat, that crosses the path of an elephant.
What must the elephant do? Squelch it – by heavens – squelch it.
Thomas Carlyle

For the great Gaels of Ireland
Are the men that God made mad,
For all their wars are merry,
And all their songs are sad.
G. K. Chesterton, *Ballad of the White Horse*

Whence does this mysterious power of Ireland come?
It is a small, poor, sparsely populated island, lapped about by British
sea-power, accessible on every side, without iron or coal. How is it that
she sways our councils, shakes our parties, and infects us with her bitter-
ness, convulses our passions, and deranges our actions? How is it she has
forced generation after generation to stop the whole traffic of the British
Empire in order to debate her domestic affairs?
Winston Churchill, Speech in the House of Commons, 1921

Everyone in Ireland seems to be unreasonable. The Irish will not recognise
that they, like every other civilised people, must adopt reasonable
methods for settling differences.
Winston Churchill, letter to Lord Riddell (1922)

I am persuaded that this is the righteous judgment of God upon those
barbarous wretches who have imbrued their hands with so much innocent
blood.
Oliver Cromwell, at Drogheda, 1649

Hell or Connaught.
Oliver Cromwell

There is no helping these half-cracky people.
Elizabeth Grant, *The Highland Lady in Ireland* (1898)

What an odd country this is; what strange tempers people have . . .
Unhappy Ireland, how much have your wild children yet to learn.
Elizabeth Grant, *The Highland Lady in Ireland*

Every Irishman has a potatoe in his head.
J.C. and A.W. Hare, *Guesses at the Truth*

This sinister country.
Henry James, quoted in Leon Edel, *The Life of Henry James*

The Irish are a fair people: they never speak well of one another.
Samuel Johnson

I do not trust . . . one single Irishman with a rifle in his hands one single
yard.
Field Marshal Lord Kitchener, 1914

. . . they're working hard to restore the old Gaelic. If they're not careful,
they'll learn to speak it and then they'll be sorry.
Stephen Leacock, *The Boy I Left Behind Me*

Kitchen Kaffir.
The London *Morning Post,* on the Irish language

For God's sake bring me a large Scotch. What a bloody awful country.
Reginald Maudling, British Home Secretary, 1970, after his first visit to
Northern Ireland

. . . the damndest race. They put so much emphasis on so many wrong
things.
Margaret Mitchell (1900-1949), *Gone With the Wind*

An Irishman is a guy who . . .
Believes salvation can be achieved by means of a weekly envelope.
Jim Murray, *L.A. Times* (1976)

For the outside world Dark Rosaleen has a sex appeal, whereas Britannia
is regarded as a maiden aunt.
Sir John Maffey, British representative in Dublin, 1945, quoted in
Jonathan Bardon, *A History of Ulster* (1992)

An Englishman thinks seated; a Frenchman, standing; an American, pacing; an Irishman, afterwards.
Austin O'Malley (1858-1932)

An Irishman is a human enthymeme – all extremes and no middle.
Austin O'Malley

The Irish are more than a frothy race. They are evaporative. They tend to lose their distinctive characteristics speedily enough.
T. Penhaligon, *The Impossible Irish* (1935)

When will Ireland be a good boy, and learn to remain quiet at home.
Punch Magazine, London (1848)

Not only are they rude, uncleanly and uncivil, they are very cruel, bloody minded, apt and ready to commit any sort of mischief.
Barnaby Rich, *A New Description of Ireland* (1610)

. . . the Irish had rather still retain this in their sluttishness, in their inhuman loathsomeness, than they would take any example from the English, either of civility, humanity, or any manner of decency.
Barnaby Rich, *A New Description of Ireland*

You would not confide free representative institutions to the Hottentots, for example . . . democracy . . . works admirably when it is confined to people who are of teutonic race.
Lord Salisbury, British Conservative leader, on Irish self-government, May 1886

Erin go bragh! A far better anthem would be Erin go bread and cheese.
Sydney Smith, *Fragment on the Irish Roman Catholic Church*

So great, and so long has been the misgovernment of Ireland, that we verily believe the empire would be much stronger, if every thing was open sea between England and the Atlantic, and if *skates* and *cod-fish* swam over the fair land of Ulster.
Sydney Smith, *Edinburgh Review* (1820)

The most ludicrous of all human objects is an Irishman ploughing. A gigantic figure – a seven-foot machine for turning potatoes into human nature, wrapt up in an immense great coat, and urging on two starved ponies, with dreadful imprecations, and uplifted shillala.
Sydney Smith, *Edinburgh Review* (1820)

. . . an English-piquing people.
Washington Post

Law and Lawyers

Chief Baron O'Grady, to a pickpocket: "You are sentenced to be whipped from the North Gate to the South Gate."
Pickpocket: "Bad luck to you, you old blackguard."
Chief Baron O'Grady: " – and back again."

Once in a noisy court session at Ballinasloe, the crier was asked by the judge to clear the court. "Now then!" he cried, "all ye blaggards that isn't lawyers must leave this instant."

"You may have observed His Lordship shaking his head while I was speaking, but gentlemen, I can assure you that there is nothing in it."
John Philpot Curran (1750-1817), to a jury

Lord Clare, to annoy Curran, once brought his pet dog to the bench. While the barrister was in full flow of his argument, the judge stooped to fondle the animal. Curran stopped his speech. When the judge looked up enquiringly at him, Curran said: "I beg your pardon. I thought your Lordship was consulting."

Earlier in Curran's career, he often crossed swords with Judge Robinson, who though he had written books, had no deep knowledge of the law. In the course of one dispute with the young lawyer, he said: "Say another word, and I'll commit you."
"If your Lordship shall do so," replied Curran, "we shall both of us have the consolation of reflecting that I am not the worst thing that your Lordship has committed."

When "Bully" Egan threatened to put the physically small John Philpot Curran in his pocket, Curran retorted: "If you do that you'll have more law in your pocket than you ever had in your head."
(This story was probably first told of the equally small but less famous lawyer Mr Caldbeck)

Lord Norbury was renowned for the severity of his judgements. One day, dining on circuit, he was asked if he would take some pickled tongue. He replied, that he did not care for pickled tongue, but if it had been hung, he would try it. Curran, sitting across the table, remarked:
"If your Lordship would only try it, it will certainly be hung."

A young barrister named Parsons was travelling with the judge Lord Norbury in his coach. As they went past a gibbet, Norbury remarked, with a chuckle: "Where would you be, Parsons, if every man had his deserts?"
"Alone in this carriage, my Lord," said Parsons.

It was Lord Norbury who remarked of Queen Caroline's alleged affair with the Dey of Algiers, "She was as happy as the Dey was long."

Sir Jonah Barrington said of Lord Norbury: "He had a hand for every man, and a heart for nobody."

An inexperienced young lawyer once addressed the court as "Gentlemen." At the end of his address, his error was pointed out to him. He immediately rose again, and adddressed the judges: "Your Honours, in my excitement, I referred to you as 'gentlemen'. I realise that that was a mistake. I beg your Honours' pardon."

Counsel, to witness: "You're a nice fellow, aren't you?"
Witness: "I am a nice fellow, and if I was not on my oath, I'd say the same about yourself."

Lord Plunkett, on being told that his successor, Chief Justice Doherty, had little or nothing to do, remarked: "Well, he is equal to it."

The law is a sort of hocus-pocus science, that smiles in yer face while it picks yer pocket
Charles Macklin (1696-1797), *Love á la Mode*

One-off Judgements

On the Abbey Theatre
The Abbey Theatre causes much more amusement than it provides.
Myles na Gopaleen (Brian O'Nolan, 1911-1966), *The Hair of the Dogma*

On Agitators
Because half a dozen grasshoppers under a fern make the field ring with
their importunate chink, while thousands of great cattle, reposed beneath
the shadow of the British oak, chew the cud and are silent, pray do not
imagine that those who make the noise are the only inhabitants of the
field . . . or that, after all, they are other than the litttle, shrivelled,
meagre, hopping, though loud and troublesome *insects* of the hour.
Edmund Burke (1729-1797), *Reflections on the Revolution in France*

On American Motion Pictures
American motion pictures are written by the half-educated for the half-
witted.
St John Ervine (1883-1971)

On Ancestors
Our ancestors are very good kind of folks; but they are the last people I
should choose to have a visiting acquaintance with.
Richard Brinsley Sheridan (1751-1816), *The Rivals*

On the Anglo-Irish
These fellows are droll enough to make your sides burst with laughing; of
mixed blood, mostly tall, strong, handsome chaps, they all wear enormous
moustaches under colossal Roman noses, give themselves the false
military air of retired colonels, travel round the country after all sorts of
pleasures, and if one makes an inquiry, they haven't a penny, are laden
with debts, and live in dread of the encumbered estates court.
Friedrich Engels, Letter to Karl Marx, May 1856

On Anglo-Irish Literature
for the most part is neither Anglo, Irish nor literature
Myles na Gopaleen (Brian O'Nolan, 1911-1966), *The Best of Myles*

On Art in Ireland
the cracked lookingglass of a servant
James Joyce (1882-1941), *Ulysses*

On a Bad Meal
God made the meat, but someone else made the cook.
Traditional

On the Baroque Style
If there is one thing I would warn you against it is the baroque style.
There you have something that lacks the sternness and strength of truly
virtuous and admirable work. It is effeminate – I would sooner have
Philipstown.
Myles na Gopaleen, *The Best of Myles* (1968)

On the Black and Tans
Men such as later in Germany would have found an instant welcome in
the Gestapo
Percy Arland Ussher, *The Face and Mind of Ireland* (1949)

On a Certain Young Lady
There's a girl in these parts –
Her name I don't sing!
But the force of her farts
Is like stones from a sling.
The Book of Ballymote, c1400

On Another Young Lady
N' fetar
cia lasa fáifea Etan,
acht rafetar Etan bán
nochon fáifea a hóenarán.
I do not know who fair Edan will sleep with, but I do know she will not
sleep alone.
Anonymous

On a Certain Young Man

Says little, thinks less, and does – nothing at all.
George Farquhar (1678-1707), *The Beaux' Stratagem*

On Children

Youth is a wonderful thing; what a crime to waste it on children.
George Bernard Shaw

On the Christian Brothers

. . . though they were not by any means uniformly savage, the worst of
them were scarcely human at all.
Flann O'Brien (Brian O'Nolan, 1911-1966), *Cruiskeen Lawn*

On Circulating Libraries

A circulating library in a town is an evergreen tree of diabolical
knowledge.
Richard Brinsley Sheridan (1751-1816), *The Rivals*

On the Climate

There is nothing wrong with our climate, except the weather.
Anonymous quotation from Donald Connery, *The Irish* (1968)

On a Conscientious Butler

Carolan, the bard, born in 1670, was well-known for his fondness for
whiskey. Whilst he was playing his harp in the house of a grand but
parsimonious lady, he saw the butler, O'Flinn, open the cellar door. He
laid his harp aside and followed the butler to request a drink. The butler
thrust him out, saying he would give him nothing, except at his mistress's
instructions. The embittered bard promptly produced a couplet:
"A shame that Hell-gates are not kept by O'Flinn!
So surly a dog would let nobody in."

On Cynics

a man who knows the price of everything and the value of nothing.
Oscar Wilde (1854-1900), *The Importance of Being Earnest*

On Critics 1
If the men of wit and genius would resolve never to complain in their works of critics and detractors, the next age would not know that they ever had any.
Jonathan Swift (1667-1745) *Thoughts on Various Subjects*

On Critics 2
Critics are like eunuchs in a harem: they know how it's done, they've seen it done every day, but they're unable to do it themselves.
Brendan Behan (1923-1964), attributed

On Diction
. . . don't sit there crooning like a bilious pigeon.
George Bernard Shaw (1856-1950) *Pygmalion*

On Drunks
A drunken man's a terrible curse,
But a drunken woman's ten times worse.

On the Duke of Wellington
. . . the licensed thug and the loud-mouthed bailiff whose victories on behalf of European reaction, and the privileges of landlords, are commemorated in the Phoenix Park.
Brendan Behan, *Confessions of an Irish Rebel*

On Economists
If all economists were laid end to end, they would not reach a conclusion.
George Bernard Shaw

On Emigrants
A Scotsman and an Irishman were conversing one day on the fortunes of emigration to the West Indies.
"Why is it," said the Scot, "That few or none of your countrymen who come here do well, while most of the Scots are prospering?"
"Because, said the Irishman, "none but fools stay in your country; and none but fools leave mine."

On an English Prison Warder
I. . . was glad that I was giving the needle to this fugh-faced, desiccated old bastard. His gills wattled in anger . . .
Brendan Behan, *Confessions of an Irish Rebel*

On Eternal Life
What man is capable of the insane self-conceit of believing that an
eternity of himself would be tolerable even to himself?
George Bernard Shaw

On the Evening Fry-Up
That fearful meal, of which the whole hotel reeks, between the hours of
six and seven-thirty.
Kate O'Brien (1897-1974), *My Ireland*

On a Fat Man
If he was cleaned out he'd make a fine duck-house.
From Alice Taylor, *To School Through the Fields* (1988)

On Fathers
Fathers should be neither seen nor heard.
Oscar Wilde

On Fiction
The good ended happily; the bad unhappily. That is what fiction means.
Oscar Wilde, *The Importance of Being Earnest*

On a Fiddler
He was a fiddler, and consequently a rogue.
Jonathan Swift

On the Film *Fort Apache*
There is enough Irish comedy to make me wish Cromwell had done a
more thorough job.
James Agee (1948)

On Fine Words
I wonder where you stole 'em?
Jonathan Swift

On Fish
I . . . wondered at a fisherman whether he ate fish. "Fish?" he replied in
astonishment. "The Irish don't eat fish. It's a poor man's food."
Peter Marshall, *Celtic Gold: A Voyage Around Ireland* (1997)

On the Foremilk of a Cow
Wasn't the foremilk of a cow or the strippings of a teapot the greatest insult you could offer anyone?
Paddy Tunney, *Where Songs Do Thunder* (1991)

On Gay Men
Get out, you low dirty things. A decent whore can't get a shilling with you around.
Meg, in Brendan Behan's *The Hostage*

On the Gentry 1
What miserable slaves are the gentry of Ireland! . . . they see Ireland only in their rent rolls, their places, their patronage and their pensions.
Theobald Wolfe Tone (1763-1798)

On the Gentry 2
The scourge of Ireland was the existence of a class who looked to be gentry living on their property, but who should have earned their bread by the work of their brow.
Anthony Trollope, *Castle Richmond*

On Grocer's Cake
The usual conglomeration of tallow, saw-dust, bad eggs, and gravel.
E. O. Somerville (1855-1949) and Violet Martin Ross (1862-1915), *The Real Charlotte*

On Happiness
Happiness is no laughing matter.
Archbishop Whately (1787-1863), *Apophthegms*

On Having an Affair
If an affair is more complication than crack, then find some friends who are as shallow and insincere as yourself.
Advice column in Belfast Sunday newspaper, quoted in Sally Belfrage, *The Crack: A Belfast Year* (1987)

On Historians – 1
Modern historians are all would-be philosophers; who, instead of relating

facts as they occurred, give us their version, or rather perversions, of them.
Lady Blessington (1789-1849), *Confessions of an Elderly Lady*

On Historians – 2
There are formidable vested interests in our huge national stock of junk and bilge, glowing with the phosphorescence of romance.
George Bernard Shaw

On History – 1
History consists, for the greater part, of the miseries brought upon the world by pride, ambition, avarice, revenge, lust, sedition, hypocrisy, ungoverned zeal, and all the train of disorderly appetites.
Edmund Burke, *Reflections Upon the Revolution in France*

On History – 2
. . . a nightmare from which I am trying to wake.
Stephen Dedalus, in James Joyce's *Ulysses*

On a Hotel in Cavan
At least it won't burn down easily.
Seán Quinn, Cavan entrepreneur, on his concrete-built hotel, quoted in John Ardagh, *Ireland and the Irish* (1994)

On a House that Seemed Small
You scarce upon the border enter
Before you're at the very centre.
Richard Brinsley Sheridan on Patrick and Mary Delany's house, Delville

On Humanity – 1
Humanity, let us say, is like people packed in an automobile which is travelling downhill without lights at terrific speed and driven by a small four year-old child. The sign-posts along the way are all marked 'Progress'.
Lord Dunsany (1878-1957)

On Humanity – 2
Most people are other people. Their thoughts are someone else's opinions,

their lives a mimicry, their passions a quotation.
Oscar Wilde, *De Profundis*

On Imagination
The most pernicious gift to the individuals who compose the talkers
instead of the writers in society.
Lady Blessington, *The Repealers*

On Irish Americans
Irish Americans are about as Irish as black Americans are African.
Bob Geldof (1954-), quoted in the London *Observer,* 22nd June 1986

On the Irish Language Movement – 1
A return to the Dark Ages.
J. P. Mahaffy (1839-1919)

On the Irish Language Movement – 2
Irish does not sell the cow.
Traditional saying

On Isadora Duncan
A woman whose face looked as if it had been made of sugar and someone
had licked it.
George Bernard Shaw

On Journalism
It keeps us in touch with the ignorance of the community.
Oscar Wilde

On Juke-Boxes
Oh dear God in Heaven, that I should find myself thousands of miles
from home, an old man at the mercy of every retarded son of a bitch who
has a nickel to drop in that bloody illuminated coal scuttle.
Oliver St John Gogarty (1878-1957), quoted in *Irish Literary Portraits*

On Junior Surgeons
Cease calling on your unqualified assistant.
Oliver St John Gogarty, to an assistant who called out 'Jesus Christ' in the
operating theatre.

On Kings
Kings are not born: they are made by universal hallucination.
George Bernard Shaw

On Landlords – 1
No, my friends, the landlords of Ireland are all of one religion – their God is Mammon and rackrents, and evictions their only morality.
Michael Davitt (1846-1906) addressing Protestant farmers in County Armagh, January 1881

On Landlords – 2
I owed the landlord two years rent; I wished I owed him more
That day the sleeky bailiff he put a notice on our door.
Geordie Hanna, *Where the Green Shamrock Grows*

On Life in the North
Nasty, British, and short.
Paul Muldoon (1951-)

On the Life to Come
Clov: Do you believe in the life to come?
Hamm: Mine was always that.
Samuel Beckett (1906-1989), *Endgame*

On Love – 1
When one is in love, one begins by deceiving oneself, and one ends by deceiving others. This is what the world calls a romance.
Oscar Wilde

On Love – 2
It is only with scent and silks and artifices that we raise love from an instinct to a passion.
George Moore (1852-1933)

On Martyrdom
Martyrdom . . . the only way in which a man can become famous without ability.
George Bernard Shaw, *The Devil's Disciple*

On a Mean Man
So mean, his soul was as narrow as a knitting-needle.
Traditional

On a Mean Woman
She'd grudge you a cold in the head.
Traditional

On Medical Science
He's a devout believer in the department of witchcraft called medical science.
George Bernard Shaw

On Mediocrities
Only mediocrities improve.
Oscar Wilde, interviewed in *The St James Gazette*, January 1893

On Men of Letters
When once the itch of literature comes over a man, nothing can cure it but the scratching of a pen.
Samuel Lover (1797-1868)

On Middle Age
We test the foreign scene
or grow too fat in banks,
salesmen for margarine,
soldiers in tanks,
the great careers all tricks,
the fine arts all my arse,
Business and politics
a cruel farce.
James Simmons, *One of the Boys* (1933)

On a Miserly Patron
I have heard
He does not bestow horses for poemss.
He gives what fits his kind:
A cow.
9th-century poet, translated by Myles Dillon in *Early Irish Literature*

On the Moyne Institute for Experimental Medicine
What a site! What an opportunity! Alas!
Terence de Vere White, *Leinster* (1968)

On Musical Amateurs
Hell is full of musical amateurs: music is the brandy of the damned.
George Bernard Shaw (1856-1950), *Major Barbara*

On Old Maids
viragos intactas
James Joyce, *Finnegans Wake*

On Oliver Cromwell
ould Oliver Crummle whose tongue is on the look out for a drop of
wather ever since he went to the lower storey
William Carleton (1798-1869), *The Irish Senachie*

On One Who Sits Around
It's another bottom he needs for the one he has he's nearly worn out,
sitting on it in the corner all day long, and shmoking and planning lies.
Eric Cross (c1905-1980), *The Tailor and Ansty*

On Opera
Sleep is an excellent way of listening to an opera.
James Stephens (1882-1953)

On People Who Do Not Read
Sad to see the sons of learning
In everlasting hell-fire burning,
While he that never reads a line
Doth in eternal glory shine.
Anonymous 9th-century Gaelic poet, quoted in Peter Haining, *Great Irish
Humorous Stories*, 1998

On People Who Turn to the Index First
There are the men who pretend to understand a book by scouting through the index; as if a traveller should go about to describe a palace when he had seen nothing but the privy.
Jonathan Swift, *On The Mechanical Operation of the Spirit*

On Pessimists
A pessimist thinks everbody as nasty as himself, and hates them for it.
George Bernard Shaw

On Philosophers
There is nothing so absurd or ridiculous that has not at some time been said by some philosopher.
Oliver Goldsmith (1728-1774)

On Plagiarism
Taking something from one man and making it worse
George Moore

On Plain-Spoken Men
The man who could call a spade a spade should be compelled to use one.
Oscar Wilde, *The Portrait of Dorian Grey*

On Plantation Settlers
From Scotland came many, and from England not a few, yet all of them generally the scum of both nations, who for debt or breaking and fleeing from justice, or seeking shelter, came thither.
Andrew Stewart, Minister of Donaghadee, 17th century

On a Play That Did Not Please
The play was a great success, but the audience was a failure.
Oscar Wilde

On the Poet Laureate
O what indignity and shame
To prostitute the Muse's name,
By flatt'ring kings whom Heav'n designed
The plague and scourge of all mankind.
Jonathan Swift, *On Poetry: A Rhapsody*

On Poets
What poet would not grieve to see
His brother write as well as he?
But rather than they should excel,
Would wish his rivals all in Hell?
Jonathan Swift, *On the Death of Dr Swift*

On Poetry
I have decided that there is no excuse for poetry . . . most of it is bad.
Nobody is going to manufacture a thousand tons of jam in the
expectation that five tons may be eatable.
Myles na Gopaleen, *The Best of Myles* (1968)

On the Police
The Polis as Polis, in this city is Null and Void.
Sean O'Casey (1880-1964), *Juno and the Paycock*

On Pornography
A taste for dirty stories may be said to be inherent in the human animal.
George Moore (1852-1933), *Confessions of a Young Man* (1888)

On Posterity
What has posterity ever done for us?
Sir Boyle Roche (1743-1807), attributed. This was echoed, knowingly or
not, by Charles J. Haughey, in a conversation on global warming: "What
about future generations?" I suggested. "What have they done for us?" was
his reply. Peter Marshall, *Celtic Gold: A Voyage Around Ireland* (1997)

On Premature Ejaculation
O why should the spurren pleasure of expectant
Woman be snaffled within a yard of the grandstand?
Austin Clarke (1896-1974), *Tiresias*

On Prison Fare
D'you mean we're getting food with our meals today?
Brendan Behan, *The Quare Fellow*

On Public Houses – 1
A drink in a club with your equals is right enough, but in a "pub", where
there may be others below your class, is quite impossible for the
self-respecting middle-class man.
Sir William Orpen (1878-1931), *Stories of Old Ireland and Myself*

On Public Houses – 2

There is no darker stain on our national honour than our public houses
. . . Old Job, that most disreputable of Jews, scraping his filthy sores on a
dunghill instead of going to a doctor, seems the patron saint of Irish
publicans.
Liam O'Flaherty (1896-1984), *The Tourist's Guide to Ireland* (1930)

On Public Persons

It is a general popular error to imagine the loudest complainers for the
public to be the most anxious for its welfare.
Edmund Burke, *Observation on a Late Publication Entitled "The Present
State of the Nation"*(1769)

On a Publican (Who was also a Poet)

You are a man who trades in small beer,
Without body or substance, and brandy
That gives your customers nightmares . . .
Bad ale you purvey every day as good porter
That your wife decants in scant quarts . . .
When yourself you pour your scarce pints,
The glasses are half-filled with froth
Aindrias MacCraith, *Small Beer,* from J. Keeffe (editor) *Irish Poems from
Cromwell to the Famine*

On Publishers – 1

Shatton and Windup
Samuel Beckett's version of Chatto and Windus, when they would not
publish his *Dream.*

On Publishers – 2

Oh Doubleday Doran
Less oxy than moron
You've a mind like a whore on
The way to Bundoran
Samuel Beckett's comment on Doubleday Doran when they rejected
Murphy (1937)

On Queen Victoria

Taking the Shamrock in her withered hand, she dares to ask Ireland for soldiers – to fight for the exterminators of their race! And the reply of Ireland comes sadly but proudly, not through the lips of the miserable little politicians who are touched by the English canker, but through the lips of the Irish people: "Queen, return to your own land; you will find no more Irishmen ready to wear the red shame of your livery."
Maud Gonne (1865-1953), quoted in Margaret Ward, *Maud Gonne, A Life* (1990)

On the Rich

After the rich, the most obnoxious people in the world are those who serve the rich.
Edna O'Brien (1932-), *August is a Wicked Month*

On Rural Housing

. . . the little white bungalows, attractive
as dandruff in the hairy armpit of the the Glen
Cathal O Searcaigh, *Bó Bhradach (A Runaway Cow)*

On Satire

Satire is a sort of glass, wherein beholders do generally discover every body's face but their own.
Jonathan Swift, Preface to *The Battle of the Books*

On Scholars

Extreme pugnacity is the essential feature of all true Irish scholars.
J. P. Mahaffy in the Dublin *Daily Express* (1899)

On the Sea

There is many a thing in the sea is not decent.
Lady Gregory (1859-1932), *The Workhouse Ward*

On Sex with a Woman

It was like chewing cold mutton.
Oscar Wilde, to Ernest Dowson, after a night with a Dieppe prostitute, 1897

On Small Businessmen

It is not by paying one's bills that one can hope to live in the memory of the commercial classes.

Oscar Wilde

On the Sons of the Nobility

. . . a weak, diseased body, a meagre countenance, and sallow complexion, are the true marks of noble blood; and a healthy, robust appearance is so disgraceful to a man of quality, that the world concludes his real father to have been a groom or coachman.

Jonathan Swift

On the Sculpture of "Molly Malone" in Dublin

The tart with the cart.

Popular saying

On Stout

A jarvey's drink.

John Joyce, father of James Joyce, quoted in Anthony Cronin, *No Laughing Matter: The Life and Times of Flann O'Brien* (1989)

On Talent

No-one can tell me who has talent, of any –
Only one thing is certain. We are too many.

W. B. Yeats, quoted remark in the Cheshire CheeseTavern

On Tea and Tea-drinkers

"The devil's plant, the tay . . . a tay-drinker, your reverence knows, will do any thing."

William Carleton, *Mysterious Doings at Slathbeg*

On Teachers

He who can does. He who cannot, teaches.

George Bernard Shaw

(Later elaborated with: He who cannot teach, trains the teachers)

On a Very Thin Person

The breath is only just in and out of him, and the grass doesn't know of him walking over it.

On the Tongue

The worst instrument attached to the human being.
Peter Flanagan, quoted in Henry Glassie, *Passing the Time* (1986)

On the Union of 1800

How did they pass the Union?
By perjury and fraud,
By slaves who sold their land for gold,
As Judas sold his God.
From a ballad of the time

On an Upstart

The rascal! That's too mild a name;
Does he forget from whence he came;
Has he forgot from whence he sprung,
A mushroom in a bed of dung;
A maggot in a cake of fat,
The offspring of a beggar's brat.
Jonathan Swift

On the Vice-Provost of Trinity College, Richard Acton

A wight inferior to none
For ponderosity of bum.
Anonymous, possibly by Jonathan Swift

On Virtue

The Trade Unionism of the married.
George Bernard Shaw, *Major Barbara*

On Work

"Intervals."
Willie Wilde (brother of Oscar) when asked what he was working at.

On the World

The whole world is in a terrible state of chassis
Sean O'Casey, *Juno and the Paycock*

On the World Outside the Mad-house

A colossal fiasco.
Samuel Beckett, *Murphy*

On a Worthy Citizen
A kind and gentle heart he had,
To comfort friends and foes;
The naked every day he clad,
When he put on his clothes.
Oliver Goldsmith (1728-1774), *Elegy on the Death of a Mad Dog*

On Would-be Wits
All human race would fain be wits,
And millions miss, for one that hits.
Jonathan Swift

Two Birds With One Stone
If one could only teach the English how to talk and the Irish how to
listen, society would be quite civilised.
Oscar Wilde

Two More Birds With One Stone
Oscar and George Bernard
Cannot be reconciled;
When I'm Wilde about Shaw,
I'm not Shaw about Wilde.
Freddie Oliver

Men

Let him go, let him tarry,
Let him sink or let him swim;
He doesn't care for me and I don't care for him;
He can go and get another, that I hope he will enjoy,
For I'm going to marry a far nicer boy.
Anonymous

Brutes never meet in bloody fray,
Nor cut each others' throats, for pay.
Oliver Goldsmith (1728-1774), *Logicians Refuted*

Cast your eyes on the habitual dram drinker, with his limbs decrepid by
the gout; his veins and bladder tortured with the stone, the great glands
full of putrifying sores; his schirrous liver swollen to an enormous load;
his dropsical belly protuberant like a tun; his asthmatic lungs panting for
breath; his shrivelled ghastly countenance discoloured into a blackish
yellow by jaundice; his hollow eyes unable to bear the light; his drivelling
looks and his wretched soul, incapable to endure its shattered habitation,
yet trembling with horror at the thought of being dispossessed.
Elizabeth Malcolm, *Ireland Sober, Ireland Free* (1886)

Even his friends could not have said
That his looks were such that she lost her head.
How else would he come by such a wife
But that ease was the alms she asked of life?
What possible use could she have at night
For dourness, dropsy, bother and blight,
A basket of bones with thighs of lead,
Knees absconded from the dead,
Fire-speckled shanks and temples whitening,
Looking like one that was struck by lightning.
Bryan Merryman (1747-1805), *The Midnight Court,* translated from
Gaelic by Frank O'Connor

When I got home I stole to my mother and in an awestruck whisper said to her, "Mamma, I think Papa's drunk."
She turned away in impatient disgust and said, "When is he ever anything else?"
George Bernard Shaw (1856-1950), Letter to Ellen Terry, June 1897

Every man over 40 is a scoundrel.
George Bernard Shaw, *Man and Superman*

He's a man of great common sense and good taste – meaning thereby a man without originality or moral courage.
George Bernard Shaw

Names

Bustler Brian O'Smellyslut, Gilly Patrick O' Belcherbuster, Malbottom
Murphy O' Meggybeard, Bridget O' Ballsey, Mightybum Mahon, Barney
Bigbelly, Niall O'Nettles, Crookedcrown Con O'Hollowgut
Names translated from the Gaelic of *The Parliament of Clan Thomas,*
c 1650

Putridpelt, Filthyfork, Dragonmaggot, Sir Donal O'Puffprattle
Further names from *The Parliament of Clan Thomas*

John O'Swill
Name for John Bull. in Pierce Fitzgerald, *Seaghán O Dighe* (18th century)

O'Trigger, O'Thunder, O'Blarney, O'Bubble, O'Screw
"Stage Irish" names from 18th-century Irish drama noted by Patrick
Rafroidi, *Irish Literature in English: The Romantic Period* (1980)

There was also a Home Rule candidate named Longbottom, which caused
a Catholic priest, himself a Home Ruler, to remark to his congregation:
"As for this Mr Long-what's-his-name, I wouldn't be dirtying my mouth
by mentioning the latter part of him."
Mark Bence-Jones, *Twilight of the Ascendancy* (1987)

Great Insulters: Oscar Wilde

Oscar Fingal O'Flahertie Wills Wilde (1854-1900) was one of the wittiest men who ever lived. By no means all his wit was reserved for insult, and even his rude remarks were redeemed from nastiness or savagery by their wit. He did not suffer from the misanthropy of Swift; indeed his too-specific love for his fellow-men proved his undoing. Wilde's wit was that of the *salon,* the theatre green room, the club; it was social and personal rather than general and political. It was essentially the wit of conversation.

His gift for epigrams is celebrated. One wonders if it was cultivated, like the speech a visitor once heard a famous statesman rehearse, which began, "Mr Speaker, I had not intended to intervene in this debate. . . " But one cannot set up in advance situations like the exchange between Wilde and Sir Lewis Morris, who wanted to be the British Poet Laureate after Tennyson, but complained:

"It is a conspiracy of silence against me – a conspiracy of silence. What should I do, Oscar?"

"Join it," said Wilde.

When a celebrated bore said to him:

"I passed your house yesterday, Oscar," he merely replied,

"Thank you so much."

Until they fell out, Wilde and the artist James McNeill Whistler were friends. Wilde admired the American's gift for repartee, while Whistler, who always rather patronised the younger man, took every opportunity to put him down. Once after some utterance of Whistler, Wilde said, "I wish I'd said that." To which his friend replied, "You will, Oscar, you will." Later, Wilde wrote of his ex-friend, "Whistler has always spelt art with a capital I." Whistler scorned Oscar's pretensions to be an art critic: "What has Oscar in common with Art? except that he dines at our tables and picks from our platters the plums for the pudding he peddles in the provinces."

In 1886, Bernard Shaw was talking to Wilde and others of starting up a socialist magazine. "You haven't told us the title," said Wilde.

"What I'd want to do is impose my own personality on the publication –
I'd call it 'Shaw's Magazine' - Shaw, Shaw, Shaw, Shaw!" He banged his
fist on the table.
"Yes," said Wilde, "and how would you spell it?"

Wilde distributed epigrams with a bountiful hand. Even though many of
them lack accuracy and depth, they always have sparkle, like "Ambition is
the last refuge of the failure", or "Women as a sex are sphinxes without
secrets." But sometimes he was devastatingly descriptive: "She has the
remains of really remarkable ugliness," and he was also capable of
damaging direct shots, like this one from a letter to *Truth* in 1890 about
Whistler: ". . . the only thoroughly original ideas I have ever heard him
express have had reference to his own superiority as a painter over
painters greater than himself." There was both a prophetic ring (for
himself) and a contemporary one (for us) in his remarks, from *An Ideal
Husband,* on sensational journalists: 'Think of their loathsome joy, of the
delight they would have in dragging you down, of the mud and mire they
would plunge you in. Think of the hypocrite with his greasy smile,
penning his leading article, and arranging the foulness of the public
placard."His last recorded rudery was to the wallpaper in the dingy hotel
room ("I am dying beyond my means") where he lay:
"One of us has to go."

Wilde as a personality was never to everyone's taste. Though he was
greatly liked in the USA, at least one American, Ambrose Bierce (no mean
satirist himself) could not stand him, and referred to him as "That
sovereign of insufferableness." But the most cruelly barbed comment was
made by his fellow-poet Algernon Swinburne, after Wilde's death: "It was
for sinners such as this Hell was created bottomless."

Offensive Phrases

Arrah, sit down on the parliamentary side of your arse for Christ's sake and don't be making a public exhibition of yourself. (*Ulysses*)

Away home and tell your mother to get married.

Bad cess to your big face.

Cheer up or I'll break your face.

A face as yella as a kite's claw.

Death on wires (an extremely thin person)

Divil send you news if (Mind your own business)

Does he swear? He'd swear a hole in an iron pot.

He needs his roof thatched.

He'd steal a halfpenny out of a blind beggarman's hat.

He's a long drink of cold water.

He's as queer as a bottle of chips.

He's that mean, he wouldn't give the steam off his piss to make ice-cream for orphans.

Her tongue would clip clouts.

I didn't think you were a west Briton (*Dubliners*)

I don't give a fish's tit.

If he doesn't conduct himself I'll wring his ear for him a yard long (*Ulysses*)

In my bollocks (Frequently used by Brendan Behan, to indicate disbelief)

It'd turn the porter sour in your guts, so it would (*Ulysses*)

It's a stepmother's breath in the air (Said of a cold day)

If you was in Hell, the Devil wouldn't piss on you.

My pity for your head.

Pog mo thón (Pronounced 'pok mo hoan', and meaning 'kiss my arse', this is one of the few Gaelic phrases known to all)

She looks as if butter wouldn't melt in her mouth; but I warrant cheese won't choke her (*The House by the Churchyard*)

She's that tight she'd skin a fart.

The back of my hand to you.

There's a smell of hay off him (said of a culchie)

They'd steal the cross from an ass's back.

Thrifty? Man, she'd skin a flea for his hide. (James Duffy, *fl* 19th century)

Will you stop acting the maggot (Don't be a nuisance)

Wind your neck down (Wise up)

You couldn't hit a hole in a ladder.

You're away in the head (crazy)

You're no more use than a chocolate teapot.

Other English-Speaking Nations

Time has triumphed, the wind has scattered all,
Alexander, Caesar, empires, cities are lost,
Tara and Troy flourished a while and fell,
And even England itself maybe, will bite the dust.
Anonymous, *Hope,* translated from Gaelic by Brendan Kennelly

The story is told of a patriotic Englishwoman in Dublin, who asked the butcher for a sheep's head, but insisted it must be English. At first the butcher said he only had Irish sheep, but then he said: "Sure I can get you an English one." He turned to his assistant. "Here, Tim, just take the brains outa that one there."

The world will see a day when England will be that low you won't be able to walk on her.
Brendan Behan (1923-1964), *The Hostage*

The English, however, are even more subtle liars in a sense than we are.
Brendan Behan, *Confessions of an Irish Rebel*

the Gael has been crying . . . for help to beat back the Anglicisation he saw dragging its slimy length along – the immoral literature, the smutty postcards, the lewd and suggestive songs were bad, yet they were mere puffs from the foul breath of paganised society. The full sewerage from the *cloaca maxima* of Anglicisation is now discharged upon us. The black devil of Socialism, hoof and horns . . .
Catholic Bulletin, 1913

One day a British airship passed over the house.
"Where is it going?" the boys asked their father.
"To hell, I hope," was the terse reply.
Anthony Cronin, *No Laughing Matter: The Life and Times of Flann O'Brien* (1989)

I never could look at an Englishman without seeing prison bars.
Maud Gonne (1865-1953), quoted in Margaret Ward, *Maud Gonne, A Life* (1990)

The English did not seek to wipe out the living culture of the native Irish. Some of them had no idea it existed.
Victoria Glendinning, *Jonathan Swift* (1998)

The English for centuries have been in the habit of coming over here and becoming more Irish than the Irish themselves.
Oliver St John Gogarty (1878-1957), *Going Native*

I defy anyone to study Irish history without getting a dislike and distrust of England.
Lady Gregory (1859-1932)

What I especially like about Englishmen is that after they have called you a thief and a liar and patted you on the back for being so charming in spite of it, they look honestly depressed if you fail to see they have been paying you a handsome compliment.
Robert Lynd (1879-1949), *Irish and English*

Thus writeth Meer Djafrit:
I hate thee, Djaun Bool,
Worse than Màrid or Afrit,
Or corpse-eating ghoul.
I hate thee like Sin,
For thy mop-head of hair,
Thy snub nose and bald chin,
And thy turkey-cock air . . .
I spit on thy clothing,
That garb for baboons.
I eye with deep loathing
Thy tight pantaloons!
I curse the cravat
That encircles thy throat,
And thy cooking-pot hat,
And thy swallow-tailed coat.
James Clarence Mangan (1803-1849), *To the Ingleezee Khafir, calling himself Djaun Bool Djenkinzon*

They think they have foreseen everything, think they have provided against everything; but the fools, the fools, the fools, they have left us our Fenian dead, and while Ireland holds these graves Ireland unfree shall never be at peace.
Pádraig Pearse (1879-1916), speech at O'Donovan Rossa's graveside in 1915

What Englishman will give his mind to politics as long as he can afford to keep a motor car?
George Bernard Shaw (1856-1950), *The Apple Cart*

You will never find an Englishman in the wrong. He does everything on principle. He fights you on patriotic principles; he robs you on business principles; he enslaves you on imperial principles.
George Bernard Shaw, *The Man of Destiny*

An asylum for the sane would be empty in America.
George Bernard Shaw

The 100% American is 99% an idiot.
George Bernard Shaw

"May God damn the English, they can't even swear without vulgarity."
John Millington Synge (1871-1909), first utterance on awakening after an anaesthetic, quoted by W. B. Yeats in a letter to John Quinn, October 1907

When a statue of Victoria was unveiled in Dublin, the Irish, surveying the plump, smug, unprepossessing features of the sovereign of England, wrote underneath it: "Ireland is Revenged".
Leonard Wibberley, *The Trouble with the Irish* (1958)

Of course, America had often been discovered before Columbus, but they always hushed it up.
Oscar Wilde (1854-1900)

It is absurd to say that there are neither ruins nor curiosities in America when they have their mothers and their manners.
Oscar Wilde

America is one long expectoration.
Oscar Wilde

Fortunately, in England at any rate, thought is not catching.
Oscar Wilde

The English country gentleman galloping after a fox – the unspeakable in pursuit of the uneatable.
Oscar Wilde, *A Woman of No Importance*

The English public takes no interest in a work of art until it is told that the work in question is immoral.
Oscar Wilde

Personalities

O brave king Brian he knew the way
To keep the peace and make the hay;
For those who were bad he'd cut off their head;
And those who were worse he killed them dead.
Traditional

. . . in this Bruce's time, for three years and a half, falsehood and famine
and homicide filled the country, and undoubtedly men ate each other in
Ireland.
Annals of Connaught, on Edward Bruce, crowned High King of Ireland in
1315

It is the coming of king James that took Ireland from us,
With his one shoe English and his one shoe Irish,
He would neither strike a blow nor would he come to terms,
And that has left misfortune on the Gaels, as long as they shall exist.
Anonymous 17th-century poet, on King James II

Seumas salach
"Dirty James", another 17th-century comment on King James II by an
anonymous disappointed Gael

Did they dare, did they dare to slay Owen Roe O'Neill?
Yes, they slew him with poison they feared to meet with steel.
Traditional song

The king of the beggars.
Epithet bestowed on Daniel O'Connell

A great poet, ye all say. But wasn't he a pagan, after all?
Mayo taxi-driver, quoted in Kate O'Brien (1897-1974), *My Ireland,* on
William Butler Yeats

The bitterest tongue that ever wagged in this island
Æ (George Russell, 1867-1935) *Open Letter to the Masters of Dublin,* on T.
M. Healy, spokesman for the Dublin employers, October 1911

the sweating, swearing, farting, belching red-faced mountain of a man
Comments by Samuel Beckett (1906-1989) on his father William Beckett,
from Deirdre Bair, *Samuel Beckett* (1978)

Dirty Darby, that was reared at a beggarwoman's paunch, many's the time
that my mother filled a gallon for you.
Padraic Colum (1881-1972), *My Irish Year,* recalling an insult heard on
the street

Here lies our good Edmund, whose genius was such
We scarcely can praise it, or blame it too much;
Who, born for the Universe, narrowed his mind,
And to party gave up what was meant for mankind.
Oliver Goldsmith (1728-1774), *Retaliation,* on Edmund Burke

And what about that lanky long maypole, Gerty Chattesworth, the witch?
– not that anyone cares tuppence if she rode on a broom to sweep the
cobwebs off the moon.
Miss Mag in Sheridan Le Fanu (1814-1873), *The House by the Churchyard*

The clever Irish have invented a new word. They are currently saying to
boycott somebody, meaning to ostracise him.
Le Figaro, Paris November 1880

Burke was a damned wrong-headed fellow, through his whole life jealous
and obstinate.
Charles James Fox, on Edmund Burke

I mistook Gogarty's white-robed maid for his wife – or mistress. I expect-
ed every poet to have a spare wife.
Patrick Kavanagh (1904-1967), *The Green Fool.* The reference cost him a
£100 fine in court for libel

an obscene scoundrel . . . who would not be hanged for no honest rope
would do it.
James Larkin (1876-1947), on the strike-breaking Belfast industrialist
Thomas Gallaher

An industrial octopus . . . a tramway tyrant, and importer of swell
cockney shopmen . . . a financial mountebank, a blood sucking vampire
. . . a pure-souled financial contortionist . . . a whited sepulchre.
James Larkin on William Martin Murphy, Dublin tramway magnate,
quoted in Arnold Wright, *Disturbed Dublin* (1914)

A scholar among rakes and a rake among scholars.
Lord Macaulay on Sir Richard Steele. The form was borrowed for Flurry
Knox in Somerville and Ross's *Irish R.M.* stories: "a gentleman among
stable-boys and a stable-boy among gentlemen."

It was only lately that I knew that Conn of the Hundred Battles lost
about two thirds of the battles for which he obtained his tremendous title.
Thomas MacNiven, letter to Charles Gavan Duffy (1844)

This gnome-like talker sparkled so recklessly that one half-dreaded he
might fall into his teacup and drown.
V. S. Pritchett, on James Stephens

If I were an Ulster Protestant, I would rather be ruled from
Constantinople by the Sultan of Turkey, than by a politician like Mr
Devlin.
F. E. Smith, on Joseph Devlin, at a speech at Cloughfern, July 12, 1912

You'd be looking at a chicken for a long time before you thought of her.
Flurry Knox on Miss Bobbie Bennett, from Edith O. Somerville and
Violet Martin Ross, *Memoirs of an Irish R.M.*

Come hither, all ye empty things,
Ye bubbles rais'd by breath of Kings;
Who float upon the tide of state,
Come hither, and behold your fate.
Let pride be taught by this rebuke,
How very mean a thing's a Duke;

From all his ill-got honours flung,
Turn'd to that dirt from whence he sprung.
Jonathan Swift (1667-1745), *A Satirical Elegy on the Death of a Late Famous General*, on the first Duke of Marlborough

Sheridan is still the same. I mean in the sense that weathercocks are still the same.
Jonathan Swift, on Dr Sheridan, father of Richard Brinsley Sheridan, in a letter to Charles Ford, 1724

When the skin shrinks on your chin, Molly Byrne, there won't be the like of you for a shrunk hag in the four quarters of Ireland.
Mary Doul in J. M. Synge (1871-1909), *The Well of the Saints*

A walking terror from beyond the hills, and she two score and five years, and two hundredweights and five pounds in the weighing scales, with a limping leg on her, and a blinded eye, and she a woman of noted misbehaviour with the old and young.
Christy in J. M. Synge, *The Playboy of the Western World*

And he a poor fellow would get drunk on the smell of a pint.
Old Mahon in J. M. Synge, *The Playboy of the Western World*

Indeed, according to popular rumour he was a man "with a bastard in every farmhouse."
Joy Melville, *Mother of Oscar* (1994), on Sir William Wilde

. . . a decidedly animal and sinister expression about his mouth, which was coarse and vulgar in the extreme, while his underlip hung and pro-truded most unpleasantly . . . Mrs Quilp was an odd sort of undomestic woman. She spent the greater part of her life in bed, and except on state occasions, she was never visible to visitors.
Mary Travers, *Florence Boyle Price: Or a Warning, by Speranza* (1863). This was a caricature of Sir William and Lady Wilde; the author had sued Sir William for rape and received a farthing damages.

. . . a pithecoid person of extraordinary sensuality and cowardice.
Frank Harris, London journalist, on Sir William Wilde, claiming to quote Dr Yelverton Tyrrell

Why are Sir William Wilde's nails so black?
Because he scratches himself.
Popular Dublin joke of the 1860s

Man coming ashore from the English ferry, after a storm: "That was the dirtiest night I ever came across."
Bystander: "What, was Sir William Wilde on board?"
Popular Dublin joke after Sir William Wilde received his knighthood

"It is only a question of premature burial, which is not such an obnoxious thing as delayed burial, which Mahaffy so obtrusively represents."
Dr Yelverton Tyrrell (1844-1914), Senior Fellow of Trinity College Dublin, referring to J. P. Mahaffy's remarks on the case of an alleged witch being buried alive

The Colebrook Hitler
Captain T. T. Verschoyle on Sir Basil Brooke, later Lord Brookeborough, 1933

Katharine Tynan, watching as Maud stunned all males she came into contact with, described how they "were flustered by her beauty and grace. But they soon got over it. . . Her aloofness must have chilled the most ardent lover."
Margaret Ward, *Maud Gonne, A Life* (1990)

Parisian demi-mondaine: "Am I not the ugliest woman in Paris, M. Wilde?"
Oscar Wilde (gallantly): "In the world, madame."
Quoted in Richard Ellman, *Oscar Wilde*

A less appetising pair I have never seen out of the Zoo, and the apes are considerably preferable to Cyril. She has the face of a golliwog.
Virginia Woolf, Letter to Vanessa Bell, on meeting Mr and Mrs Cyril Connolly in a house in Ireland, May 1934

She had to choose (perhaps all women must) between broomstick and distaff and she has chosen the broomstick – I mean the witches' hats.
W. B. Yeats (1865-1939), on Maud Gonne, letter to Olivia Shakespear (1923)

Places

Stroke City
Reference to Derry/Londonderry, quoted in Peter Marshall, *Celtic Gold: A Voyage Around Ireland* (1997)

Knockamore, both mean and poor,
A church without a steeple;
Where bitches and whores look over half-doors,
To scoff at decent people.
Anonymous author, quoted in Bryan Macmahon, *Here's Ireland* (1970)

Vain Armagh city, I did thee pity,
Thy meats' rawness, and thy women's nakedness.
Italian Friar, quoted by Fynes Morison, *Itinerary* (1516-17)

A mean, miserable, beggarly town. And since they've got the sugar factory there's no standing them.
Leix man on Carlow, quoted in Frank O'Connor, *Irish Miles* (1947)

Mayo – God help us
Heinrich Böll, *Irish Journal* (1937)

. . . one of the most barren, uncouth and desolate counties that could be seen, fit only to confine rebels and ill spirits into.
Sir Arthur Chichester, Lord Deputy of Ireland, on the Donegal landscape, 1607

As the deluge subsides and the waters fall short we shall see the dreary steeples of Fermanagh and Tyrone emerging once again.
Winston Churchill, Speech in the House of Commons, London, February 1922

O the bricks they will bleed and the rain it will weep,
And the damp Lagan fog lull the city to sleep;

It's to hell with the future and live on the past;
May the Lord in His mercy be kind to Belfast.
Maurice James Craig (1919-), *Ballad to a Traditional Refrain*

The landscape of hell in *The Third Policeman* is, as Aidan Higgins has
pointed out, unmistakeably that of the Irish midlands. . . Hell is situated
somewhere near Tullamore.
Anthony Cronin, *No Laughing Matter: The Life and Times of Flann
O'Brien* (1989)

The town of Raphoe appears to have little to engage the attention.
J. C. Curwen, *Observations on the State of Ireland* (1818)

Kilkenny . . . such a den of pick-pockets, that I think the thieves in
Drogheda are saints to them.
John Dunton, *The Life and Errors of John Dunton, Citizen of London*
(1818)

Belfast . . . as uncivilised as ever – savage black mothers in houses of dark
red brick, friendly manufacturers too drunk to entertain you when you
arrive.
E. M. Forster, letter to T. E. Lawrence

I will live in Ringsend
With a red-headed whore
And the fanlight gone in
Where it lights the hall-door.
Oliver St John Gogarty (1878-1957)

O stony grey soil of Monaghan
The laugh from my love you thieved;
You took the gay child of my passion
And gave me your clod-conceived.
Patrick Kavanagh (1904-1967), *Stony Grey Soil*

Drumquin, you're not a city: you're the town that God forgot
And the man that sang your praises was entitled to be shot
For the finest land in Longfield wouldn't grow a decent whin,

And a goat would die with hunger on the hills above Drumquin
Felix Kearney, extempore addition to his celebrated *The Hills Above Drumquin,* quoted in Paddy Tunney, *Where Songs Do Thunder* (1991)

Anything to escape from fucking Cork.
Brendan Kennelly (1936-), *Cromwell*

This is a dead ould place . . . the shopkeepers here has us fleeced: butter is threepence a pound cheaper in Arklow.
Gorey resident, quoted in Bryan Macmahon, *Here's Ireland* (1970)

As early as 1866 G. S. Measom wrote of it in his MGWR Guide as having "a strong fish-like smell, and altogether so dirty and uncomfortable, that the tourist will not feel inclined to linger in the town any longer than is necessary."
Fergus Mulligan, *One Hundred and Fifty Years of Irish Railways* (1983), on Drogheda

"The guidebook says it's rebuilt in the original style."
". . . the original style or an original style?"
Conversation on Tuam Cathedral, in Frank O'Connor, *Irish Miles* (1947)

A local councillor, in opposing Sunday opening for the local cinemas, declared that he wasn't going to see Skibbereen turned into another Paris.
Sean O'Faolain (1900-1991), *An Irish Journey* (1940)

. . . a fit receptacle for all the savage beasts of the land.
Sir John Perrott, Lord Deputy of Ireland, on Ulster, 1584

Its animation is its sole charm.
Stephen Rynne, *All Ireland* (1956), on Galway

A good place to commit suicide in.
Skibbereen landlady, recorded in Peter Somerville-Large, *The Coast of West Cork* (1975)

High church, low steeple,
Dirty town, proud people.
Jonathan Swift (1667-1745) on Newry

The filthy town of Knoctopher
Richard Twiss, *A Tour in Ireland* (1775)

A minister said to me, whose congregation had been bombed . . . if he
could get the people entirely out of the way, he would be happy if the
Germans would come and bomb the place flat.
Dr J. B. Woodburn, commenting on Belfast housing, after the blitz of
1941, quoted in Jonathan Bardon, *A History of Ulster* (1992)

Great Insulters: George Bernard Shaw

Shaw (1856-1950) is one of the most accomplished masters of abuse in the English language. Sustained by an unshakable self-esteem, with apparently effortless ease he could demolish several targets at once as in: "With the single exception of Homer, there is no eminent writer, not even Sir Walter Scott, whom I can despise so entirely as I despise Shakespeare when I measure my mind against his . . . it would positively be a relief to me to dig him up and throw stones at him. . . " Aphorisms were spun off by Shaw like snowflakes:

"It is dangerous to be sincere unless you are also stupid."

"When a stupid man is doing something that he is ashamed of, he always declares that it is his duty."

"A perpetual holiday is a good working definition of hell."

Like Swift, Shaw could muster indignation against his fellow-men, but unlike Swift, his fury often had a contrived feel:

"Man remains, what he has always been; the cruellest of all the animals, and the most elaborately and fiendishly sensual." Nevertheless, he was capable of swift and deadly repartee. Once in a train, he objected to a lady smoking, saying it would make him sick.

"I'll have you know that I am one of the Directors' wives," said the lady. "Madam," said Shaw, "I do not care if you are the Director's only wife, I should still be sick."

On another occasion, responding to a lady's invitation card saying that on such and such a date she would be "At Home", he responded: "So shall I. G.B.S."

His view of his fellow-countrymen was not very high; in "John Bull's Other Island" (1907) he wrote: "An Irishman's heart is nothing but his imagination." But his opinion of everyone else was not much better: "Why was I born with such contemporaries?"

Like most great insulters, Shaw also had to endure more than a few barbs sent his way, as readers of this book will see. Perhaps his most bitter detractor was the less successful playwright Henry Arthur Jones, who among many other rude comments, referred to him as a "fiendish homunculus germinated outside lawful procreation."

Politics and Politicians

1 The pomp of courts and powers of Kings,
2 I prize above all earthly things,
3 I love my country, and the King
4 Above all men his praise I sing;
5 The royal banners are displayed
6 And may success the standard aid.

1 I fain would banish far from hence,
2 The rights of man and common sense.
3 Destruction to his hated reign,
4 That plague of Princes, Thomas Paine.
5 Defeat and ruin seize the cause
6 Of France, her liberties, and laws.

Anonymous Jacobin poem published in Belfast, 1798. This is a trick
poem, like many by the earlier (and politically very different) Jacobites.
Lines 1, 2, etc of each verse should be read in sequence.

Talking potatoes
Gibe against Irish MPs at Westminster, made by a Scottish member,
around 1860, quoted in Richard Mullen, *Anthony Trollope* (1990)

The silent sisters
Contemporary description of the three Fianna Fáil women TDs, 1937

If either found a bank-note in the street, Haughey would pocket it,
whereas Fitzgerald would lose it.
Dublin joke on Charles Haughey and Garrett Fitzgerald, political rivals

You lying BBC: you're photographing things that aren't happening.
Anonymous Belfast woman to a BBC camera team, quoted in Matthew
Parris, *Scorn* (1994)

He is a schizoid split six ways, two of them very decent people, two awful,
and two quite unpredictable.
Anonymous comment on the Rev. Ian Paisley, quoted in John Ardagh,

Ireland and the Irish (1994)
Hell is not hot enough nor eternity long enough to hold the Fenians.
Catholic bishop in the 1860's, quoted in Bryan Macmahon, *Here's Ireland*
(1970)

It remained for the twentieth century and the capital city of Ireland to see
an oligarchy of four hundred masters deciding openly on starving one
hundred thousand people, and refusing to consider any solution except
that fixed by their pride . . . If you had between you collectively a
portion of human soul as large as a threepenny bit, you would have sat
night and day with the representatives of labour. . .
Æ (George Russell, 1867-1935), *Open Letter to the Masters of Dublin,*
October 7, 1911

"Billy, it's a blessing that you're a teetotaller for you're coarse enough
when you're sober."
Tribute to Billy Grant, Northern Labour politician, from a colleague,
quoted in Jonathan Bardon, *A History of Ulster* (1992)

Meg: They say he's a very clever man. They say he can speak seven
languages.
Pat: It's a terrible pity that English or Irish are not among them, so we'd
know what he was saying at odd times.
Brendan Behan (1923-1964), *The Hostage,* on President de Valera

He engaged in a breathless series of public relations gimmicks,
culminating in his unveiling a plaque to himself in Castlebar, a gesture
which made even his most ardent and closest political colleagues cringe.
Vincent Browne, *Magill* Magazine, June 1981, on Charles Haughey

I have in general no very exalted opinion of the virtue of paper
government.
Edmund Burke (1729-1797), *On Conciliation With America* (1775)

At last dying in the last dyke of prevarication.
Edmund Burke, in the trial of Warren Hastings (1789)

A perfect democracy is therefore the most shameless thing in the world.
Edmund Burke, *Reflections on the Revolution in France* (1790)

Posterity will ne'er survey
A finer grave than this:
Here lie the bones of Castlereagh –
Stop, traveller and —.
Lord Byron, on Viscount Castlereagh

The intellectual eunuch, Castlereagh.
Lord Byron

The most nefarious conspiracy that has ever been hatched against a free
people.
Sir Edward Carson (1854-1935), on the Home Rule Bill, September 1911

The Irish have a genius for conspiracy rather than for government.
Winston Churchill

He regards the Dáil as something at best to be tolerated.
Frank Cluskey, Speech in Dáil Eireann, on Charles Haughey

The long hoor.
Michael Collins (1890-1922), *The Path to Freedom,* on Eamonn de Valera

The foulest brood that ever came into Ireland.
James Connolly (1868-1916) on Joseph Devlin's Board of Erin (1906)

Milking a cow.
Pat Cox MEP, on Ireland's earlier attitude to the European Community,
quoted in *The Irish Times,* April 1992

The allegation that he would have joined the British Army in 1916 had
he not missed a train at Mallow, was one of the Dáil's running jokes.
Anthony Cronin, *No Laughing Matter: The Life and Times of Flann
O'Brien* (1989), referring to Sean MacEntee

The Forty Thieves
Title of a pamphlet on the subject of Government Boards, by Michael
Davitt (1846-1906)

a damned wrong-headed fellow
Charles James Fox, on Edmund Burke

. . . he is like trying to pick up mercury with a fork.
David Lloyd George, British Prime Minister, on Eamonn de Valera

That sink of acidity
Oliver St John Gogarty (1878-1957), on Sir Edward Carson

Uncle Tim's Cabin
Oliver St John Gogarty on Tim Healy's occupancy of the Vice-regal Lodge

In Ireland an obscure prejudice, born of slave teaching, surrounds the
words Socialism and Communism, which even the clear thought and
noble life and death of James Connolly failed to entirely dispatch.
Maud Gonne (1865-1953), letter to Æ (George Russell) 1923

unmasked, he is sinking into an unhonoured grave, almost execrated by
the public he deluded.
Elizabeth Grant, *The Highland Lady in Ireland*, on the death of Daniel
O'Connell, April 1847

If this is liberty, the lexicographers have deceived us.
Arthur Griffith (1871-1922), on the Home Rule Bill, April 1912

I will not reply to any damned Englishman in this Assembly.
Arthur Griffith, remark in Dáil Eireann, to Erskine Childers

It is a very dangerous thing to approach an expiring cat.
Sir William Harcourt, Letter to William Gladstone, November 1890, on
Charles Stewart Parnell

Oft have I wonder'd, that on Irish ground
No poisonous reptiles ever yet were found;
Reveals the secret strands of Nature's work,
She sav'd her venom to create a Burke.
Warren Hastings, on Edmund Burke (his prosecutor, 1788)

. . . the official economist, like Diogenes, clutching his lantern, peering into the statistical gloom and searching for some faint sign of the longed-for upturn.
Charles Haughey, Speech to the Dublin Society of Chartered Accountants, 1975

If a farmer wanted someone to blow his nose some Hon Member would get up and raise the question in this House, and a man would be appointed not only to blow the farmer's nose but to wipe it for him.
Tommy Henderson, Independent Unionist member at Stormont, in the 1920s

Stormont ended quietly, almost in anti-climax. In the restaurant a Unionist Senator looked towards a table of MPs and Ministers, "Captains and Kings," he muttered. Then he added, "My foot."
Henry Kelly, *The Irish Times* (March 1972), on the last day of the Stormont Parliament

A slightly constitutional party
Sean Lemass (1899-1971), comment on Fianna Fáil, 1928

I return your seasonal greetings card with contempt. May your hypocritical words choke you and may they choke you early in the New Year, rather than later.
Professor Kennedy Lindsay, Stormont Vanguard party member, to Dr Garrett Fitzgerald, quoted in the *Irish Times*

Of all the bad men I ever was acquainted with he is the worst.
Lord Longueville on Arthur O'Connor (1763-1852)

Whilst envenomed politicians in the Ulster parliament are voting themselves power to use torture and capital punishment against citizens whom they forbid to defend themselves while they scarcely attempt to protect them from massacre, some of their own partisans in Belfast carry wholesale murder to refinements of barbarity hardly surpassed in Armenia and Constantinople.
The *Manchester Guardian*, April 1922

John Taylor described us as the WC, and I said we'd flush away his certainties.
Monica McWilliams, of the Northern Ireland Women's Coalition

There'll be no more nibbling at my leader's bum.
P. J. Mara, press officer of Fianna Fáil, 1984

Next to the British government, the worst enemy Ireland ever had – or rather the most fatal friend.
John Mitchel (1815-1875), *The Last Conquest of Ireland*, on Daniel O'Connell

Last night I toss'd and turned in bed,
But could not sleep – at length I said,
I'll think of Viscount C - stl - r - gh,
And of his speeches. That's the way.
Thomas Moore (1779-1852), *Insurrection of the Papers*, on Lord Castlereagh

If I saw Mr Haughey buried at midnight at a cross-roads, with a stake driven through his heart – politically speaking – I should continue to wear a clove of garlic round my neck, just in case.
Conor Cruise O'Brien (1917-), in the London *Observer*, October 1982

He is a liar in actions and in words. His life is a living lie. He is a disgrace to his species. . . His life, I say again, is a living lie. He is the most degraded of his species and kind; and England is degraded in tolerating or having upon the face of our society a miscreant of his abominable, foul and atrocious nature.
Daniel O'Connell (1775-1847), in a public speech in Dublin, in 1835, on Benjamin Disraeli. Denying any anti-semitic feeling, O'Connell went on to suggest Disraeli's descent from the impenitent thief who died upon the Cross, "whose name, I verily believe must have been Disraeli." The victim made a spirited reply by letter, addressing O' Connell as a yahoo, and suggesting: "If it had been possible for you to act like a gentleman, you would have hesitated before you made your foul and insolent comments." Disraeli said of O'Connell on another occasion, "He has committed every crime that does not require courage."

The disease . . . manifests itself among our politicians principally in the belief that Ireland is a living being; a woman in fact. This woman is claimed by them to be a very beautiful creature and very unfortunate . . . They love her under different names and it appears that the wench has a great variety of aliases; in other words she has changed her lover more often than she should if she wanted to lead a quiet life. At one moment she is Caitlín ni Houlihain, at another Roisin Dubh, at another the Old Woman of Beara. She changes her name to suit the particular character of the politician that courts her.
Liam O'Flaherty, *The Tourist's Guide to Ireland* (1930)

As he rose like a rocket, so he fell like the stick.
Thomas Paine, on Edmund Burke

This Romish man of sin is now in Hell.
Rev Ian Paisley, on the death of Pope John XXIII, June 1963

Moo, moo, moo, moo.
Ian Paisley, Jnr, when Monica McWilliams of the Northern Ireland Women's Coalition was trying to speak about the BSE crisis.

My policy is not a policy of conciliation, but a policy of retaliation.
Charles Stewart Parnell (1846-1891), House of Commons, 1877, quoted in *Dictionary of National Biography*

There is no subject about which Mr Parnell is so ignorant as that of Irish history.
Thomas O'Connor Power, *The Anglo-Irish Quarrel: A Plea for Peace* (1880)

The brogue-tongued Captain plods along, swamping Ministerial time and patience by the dreary drip of words.
Punch magazine, London, on Captain James Craig (later Lord Craigavon)

Mr Speaker, I smell a rat; I see him forming in the air and darkening the sky; but I'll nip him in the bud.
Sir Boyle Roche (1743-1807), attributed, in Barrington's *Personal Sketches*. This has also been attributed to the barrister, Serjeant MacMahon.

Grattan, after all, was no great thing – full of wit and fire and folly. . . a sentimental harlequin.
Samuel Rogers on Henry Grattan

Gladstone . . . spent his declining years trying to guess the answer to the Irish Question; unfortunately whenever he was getting warm the Irish secretly changed the Question.
W.C. Sellar and R.J. Yeatman, *1066 And All That* (1930)

He knows nothing and thinks he knows everything. That points clearly to a political career.
George Bernard Shaw (1856-1950) *Major Barbara*

From the silence which prevails, I conclude Lauderdale has been making a joke.
Richard Brinsley Sheridan (1751-1816)

Mr Sheridan: Where, o where, shall we find a more foolish knave or a more knavish fool than this?
Hon. Member: Hear! Hear!
Apocryphal exchange from the House of Commons

Thomas Sheridan, son of Richard Brinsley Sheridan (see Personalities) aspired to enter the London Parliament. He said to his father: "Many men who are called great patriots in the House of Commons are really great humbugs. For my part, when I get into Parliament, I will pledge myself to no party, but write upon my forehead in legible characters: 'To Be Let.'"
His father replied: "And under it, Tom, write 'Unfurnished.'"

Sheridan was notoriously short of money, and was to die in debt. Having just bought a house in Savile Row, London, he met Lord Guildford, and said, "Now, my dear lord, everything is carried on in my house with the greatest regularity; everything, in short, goes just like clockwork."
"Ah," said his lordship, "tick, tick, tick, I suppose."

Whoever could make two ears of corn or two blades of grass to grow upon a spot of ground where only one grew before would deserve better of mankind and do more essential service to his country than the whole race of politicians put together.
– Jonathan Swift (1667-1745)

For 25 years the Irish people have been gradually drawn into the personality of Charles J. Haughey, to the point where – personal relationships apart – we have practically no other means of relating to each other.
John Waters, *The Irish Times*, 1992

Tandy . . . was the ugliest man I ever gazed on. He had a dark, yellow, truculent-looking countenance, a long drooping nose, rather sharpened at the point, and the muscles of his face formed two cords at each side of it.
J. E. Walsh, *Sketches of Ireland Sixty Years Ago* (1852), on Napper Tandy

There is hardly a person in the House of Commons worth painting, though many of them would be better for a little white-washing.
Oscar Wilde (1854-1900)

Schools and Learning

A wretched uncharactered itinerant derives a scanty and precarious existence by wandering from parish to parish and opening a school in some ditch covered with heath and furze to which the inhabitants send their children to be instructed by the miserable breadless being who is nearly as ignorant as themselves.
Sir John Carr, *The Stranger in Ireland* (1806), on hedge-schoolmasters

Popular education was bringing the graffito lower on the walls.
Oliver St John Gogarty (1878-1957), *As I Was Going Down Sackville Street*

Nothing trivial, I hope.
J. P. Mahaffy (1839-1919), on learning of the illness of the Provost of Trinity (whose post he himself was to hold)

When Mahaffy, well-known for exaggeration, remarked among a group of Trinity dons that he had only been beaten once as a boy, and that was for telling the truth, George Salmon observed: "It certainly cured you, Mahaffy."

There was teaching us as schoolmistress, a woman who was as grey as a badger, with two tusks of teeth hanging down over her lip, and, if she wasn't cross, it isn't day yet.
Maurice O'Sullivan, *Twenty Years A-Growing*, translated by Moya Llewelyn Davies and George Thomson

Greek scholars are privileged men; few of them know Greek, and most of them know nothing else.
George Bernard Shaw (1856-1950)

The Irish in general have obtained a mediocrity of knowledge, between learning and ignorance, not adequate to the purposes of common life.
Richard Twiss, *A Tour in Ireland* (1775)

Sports

. . . an average player who came into the game when it was short of
personalities. He's not fit to lace my boots as a player.
George Best, on Kevin Keegan

A denationalising plague carrying on through winter the work of ruin that
cricket was doing throughout the summer.
Michael Cusack, 1864, on Rugby

Rugby Union . . .
A parody of homosexual aggression.
Paul Durcan (1944-), *The Two Little Boys at the Back of the Bus*

Wanderers, Dublin's oldest rugby club, has been described more than once
as the club of the Church and the Army: the wags added
" . . . unfortunately the wrong Church and the wrong Army."
Gemma Hussey, *Ireland Today* (1994)

Baseball has the great advantage over cricket of being sooner ended.
George Bernard Shaw (1856-1950)

I do not play cricket, because it requires me to assume such indecent
positions.
Oscar Wilde (1854-1900)

The Struggle for Independence and After

Sacred to the memory of
William Orr
who was offered up at Carrickfergus
on Saturday, the 14th October 1797,
an awful sacrifice to Irish freedom
on the Altar of British Tyranny,
by the hands of Perjury,
Thro' the Influence of Corruption and
the Connivance of Partial Justice!!
From memorial cards circulated clandestinely in 1797

Mangling done here.
Notice put up by supporters of the 1798 Insurrection at John Beresford's
house, Dublin, where suspected rebels were held and tortured

With a restraint and poise to which, I say, history will find few parallels,
His Majesty's Government never laid a violent hand upon them though at
times it would have been quite easy and quite natural, and we left the
Dublin Government to frolic with the Germans and later with the
Japanese representatives to their hearts' content.
Winston Churchill, British Prime Minister, victory speech, May 1945

Pat: Where the hell were you in nineteen-sixteen when the real fighting
was going on?
Meg: I wasn't born yet.
Pat: You're full of excuses.
Brendan Behan (1923-1964), *The Hostage*

I am prouder to stand here today in the traitor's dock than to fill the
place of my right honourable accusers.
Sir Roger Casement (1864-1916), at his trial

We've been waiting seven hundred years; you can have the seven minutes.
Michael Collins, to the English delegates, on arriving late at Dublin
Castle, January 16, 1922, quoted in Tim Pat Coogan, *Michael Collins*
(1990)

Red, white and blue,
The dirty English crew.
Green, white and yella,
The brave Irish fella.
Children's song, quoted in Hugh Leonard (1926-), *Home Before Night*

We see in their regime a thing of evil incarnate.
Terence MacSwiney (1879-1920), August 1920

I draw the line when I hear the gunman blowing about dyin' for the
people, when it's the people that are dyin' for the gunmen!
Sean O'Casey (1880-1964), *The Shadow of a Gunman*

Transport and Travel

One minister told his congregation he "would rather join a company for theft and murder than the Ulster Railway Company, since its business is sending souls to the devil at the rate of 6d a piece", and that every blast of the railway whistle was "answered by a shout in Hell."
Jonathan Bardon, *A History of Ulster* (1992). The railway's offence was running Sunday trains

"A modest pothole," he said.
"That is a pothole?"
"The roads of Ireland are built round them."
Eamonn Casey, Bishop of Galway, quoted in Annie Murphy, *Forbidden Fruit* (1993)

. . . careful men took the precaution to put their teeth in their pockets before embarking.
The Rev. J. G. Digges, on the Cavan & Leitrim Light Railway, quoted in Fergus Mulligan, *One Hundred and Fifty Years of Irish Railways*

One day an American visitor was waiting for a train and complaining loudly about the weather, the lack of stimulation in the town, the state of the world and sundry other matters. Finally he asked for directions to the "washroom". Lindsay indicated the large Gentlemen sign further up the platform saying: "Pay no attention to that, just go on in."
Fergus Mulligan, *One Hundred and Fifty Years of Irish Railways* (1983), on Alec Lindsay, stationmaster at Lisbellaw, Great Northern Railway of Ireland

. . . an old sea-captain who used, before he retired, to run the boats from Kingstown to Holyhead. Once the Lord Lieutenant and his wife were on board, and the sea was a thousand devils loose. Fifteen minutes out, just by the Kish lighthouse, her ladyship sent up a message that the captain must turn back the ship. The captain looked at the messenger. He looked at the waves, high as the mast. He looked down at the troughs, deep as hell.

"Back!" he roared. "Turn back? I never turn back. Tell her ladyship from me that the word is Hell or Holyhead."
Sean O'Faolain, *An Irish Journey* (1940)

Women

Three ladies who had been eminent in the Republican movement set out
to embarrass President Cosgrave, who was due to visit Mountjoy Prison,
by laying themselves on iron bedsteads at the prison gate. As the President
arrived, they accused him of being a traitor and dared him to arrest them.
He replied: "I may be a traitor but I am not a collector of antiques."
Apocryphal tale

Coming in with a Yank on a jeep.
All the girls in Derry think it's cheap.
With their clothes up to their bum,
And their chewing Yankee gum,
Coming in with a Yank on a jeep.
World War II song

I wish Adam had died with all his ribs in his body.
Dion Boucicault (1822-1890)

A woman is but an animal, and not of the highest stock.
Edmund Burke (1729-1797)

"O grandson of Conn, O Cormac," said Cairbre, "how do you distinguish
women?"
"Not hard to tell," said Cormac. "I distinguish them, but I make no
difference amongst them.
They are crabbed as constant companions
haughty when visited,
lewd when neglected . . .
stubborn in a quarrel, not to be trusted with a secret . . .
Better to whip than to humour them,
Better to scourge than to gladden them . . .
They are moths for sticking to you,
They are serpents for cunning.'
The Instructions of King Cormac MacAirt, 3rd century AD

I hate you
Because having slept with me
You left me.
Paul Durcan (1944-), *Felicity in Turin*

I can see Kitty waiting for me at the end of the long boreen:
I am about to drop dead but she is serene.
Paul Durcan, *Sam's Cross*

Of their cleanliness I will not speak.
Luke Gernon, *A Discourse of Ireland* (1620)

"No," his da said, "never call a woman by a name like that, not even if
she was a right old hoor."
Hugh Leonard (1926-) *Home Before Night*

She's the sort of woman who lives for others – you can always tell the
others by their hunted expression.
C.S. Lewis (1898-1963), *The Screwtape Letters*

. . . MacCooey was not fit for a seat at her table,
In the kitchen with buttermilk the poet she stabled,
While the boor, to all learning and culture contrary,
Gulped wine in the parlour with that Cock-eyed Mary.
Art MacCubhthaigh (*fl* 18th century), *Cock-Eyed Mary*, translated from
Gaelic by Críostóir O'Flynn, in *Irish Comic Poems* (1995)

Your neighbour's poor, and you, it seems, are big with vain ideas,
Because, Inagh! you've got three cows – one more, I see, than she has.
That tongue of yours wags more at times than Charity allows,
But if you're strong, be merciful, great Woman of Three Cows!
Now there you go! You still, of course, keep up your scornful bearing,
And I'm too poor to hinder you; but, by the coat I'm wearing,
If I had but four cows myself, even though you were my spouse,
I'd thwack you well to cure your pride, my Woman of Three Cows.
James Clarence Mangan (1803-1849), *The Woman of Three Cows*, from
Gaelic, author unknown. His version of the poem was itself insulted by
Críostóir O'Flynn as "colloquial doggerel" and "a jingle", in the
introduction to *Irish Comic Poems* (1995)

Our sun's eclipse, sure, is no wonder,
And all the ills we labour under.
For artful women are our ruin,
And all we suffer is their doing.
Brian Merriman (*d*1805), *The Midnight Court*, translated by Arland Ussher

My only books were women's looks, and folly's all they taught me.
Thomas Moore (1779-1852)

The wives of the Irish lords . . . often drink till they be drunken, or at least till they void urine in full assembly of men.
Fynes Morison, *An Itinerary* (published 1735 but written 1516-17)

Women are the very devil for plámás . . . they must be fawning on you every time they come across you
Maurice O'Sullivan, *Twenty Years A-Growing* (1936), translated by Moya Llewelyn Davies and George Thomson

If you haven't met my friend, Frank Prejudice, he's the fellow who rang the Late Late Show the night the new women deputies were on it, and asked who was minding their children while they were on television.
Maire Geoghegan Quinn, speech to Fianna Fáil women, May 1993

The fickleness of the women I love is only equalled by the infernal constancy of the women who love me.
George Bernard Shaw (1856-1950)

Many men (including, it is whispered, the President) think that a woman cuts a more fitting and more useful figure when darning the rents in her husband's socks by the fireside than she could hope to cut in a Parliamentary assembly.
Sunday Independent, February 1937

A very little wit is valued in a woman, we are as pleased with a few words spoken plain by a parrot.
Jonathan Swift (1667-1745), *Thoughts Upon Various Subjects*

Two women seldom grow intimate but at the expense of a third person.
Jonathan Swift

A dead wife under the table is the best goods in a man's house.
Jonathan Swift

As to the natural history of the Irish species, they are only remarkable for
the thickness of their legs, especially those of the plebeian females.
Richard Twiss, *A Tour in Ireland* (1775)

The tyranny of the weak over the strong. It is the only tyranny that ever
lasts.
Oscar Wilde (1854-1900); his view of the history of women.

Twenty years of romance makes a woman look a ruin, but twenty years of
marriage makes her look something like a public building.
Oscar Wilde

Women's styles may change, but their designs remain the same.
Oscar Wilde

She who hesitates is won.
Oscar Wilde

The complexion of the women, which in general in the cabins of Ireland
has a near resemblance to that of a smoked ham.
Arthur Young, *A Tour in Ireland* (1780)

Great Insulters: Oliver St John Gogarty

Doctor, poet, politician – Gogarty (1878-1957) was a man of many parts. One of the things that united them all was his frequently vituperative wit. He could not resist a barbed shaft. Soon after the death of his friend the talented but sometimes facile Irish artist Sir William Orpen, he said to Orpen's closest friend: "Ah, our artist! Now that he's under the sod he's got beneath the surface for the first time."

Writing to Lady Leslie about the guests for the Tailteann Games in 1924, he said: "Lady Conyngham is giving them all lunch at Slane for a visit to Newgrange, which is described as a pre-Christian cemetery, but this would be misleading except to us who know that the suggestion of subsequent Christianity is unfounded."

He had a hot time in politics (his escape from shooting by swimming the Liffey is famous). A senator in the Irish Parliament, he did not have a high opinion of politicians as a breed: "In cases where the villages are overgrown and turned into towns, the village idiot is not so recognisable. He may have been elected to Parliament." In a Senate speech in 1935, he was laying into the President with a fine ferocity, when he was called to order: "I have the greatest pleasure in withdrawing my comparison between the criminal Lynchehaun and President de Valera. I was only comparing the strength of their bodyguards, but I will alter it and say that the President is the greatest national fiasco since Jem Roche." Jem Roche was an Irish heavyweight who was knocked out in 88 seconds in a title bout in Dublin in 1908. Later, Gogarty was to refer to de Valera as "the laugh in mourning", and once wrote: "We rose to bring about Eutopia, But all we got was Dev's myopia."

Gogarty himself was often the object of attack, notably when he was sued for libel by Henry Morris Sinclair in 1937. Sinclair's counsel said: "Dr Gogarty has vilified the living and the dead in a pen dipped in the scourgings of a putrid and amoral mind. He has pursued the plaintiff with savagery and ghoulishness which could only fit in with the aberrations of an amoral mind in a pot-boiling scurrility run for the private gain of the author." Losing the case was one of the causes of Gogarty's removing from Ireland to the United States.

He did record with grace one occasion when he himself was put down in the best Irish manner. As a young man, on a bus travelling to Connemara, he said to the man beside him, "in my best social accent. . . 'It is the most extraordinary weather for this time of year.'
He replied: 'Ah, it isn't this time of year at all.'"

Index of Authors Quoted